Research Report No 116

Kojo Sebastian Amanor

LAND, LABOUR AND THE FAMILY IN SOUTHERN GHANA

A Critique of Land Policy under Neo-Liberalisation

D1612900

Nordiska Afrikainstitutet
Uppsala 2001

This report was commissioned and produced under the auspices of the Nordic Africa Institute's programme "The Political and Social Context of Structural Adjustment in Sub-Saharan Africa". It is one of a series of reports published on the theme of structural adjustment and socio-economic change in contemporary Africa.

Programme Co-ordinator and Series Editor: Adebayo Olukoshi

Indexing terms

Land policy
Land tenure
Labour
Family
Kinship
Ghana

Language checking: Elaine Almén

ISSN 1104-8425
ISBN 91-7106-468-0
© the author and Nordiska Afrikainstitutet 2001
Printed in Sweden by Elanders Digitaltryck AB, Göteborg 2001

Contents

Introduction

In recent years research on land reform has undergone a resurgence mirroring economic transformations in developing countries and the former Soviet bloc brought about by economic liberalisation and structural adjustment. These seek to bring about new institutional arrangements and reforms that give a greater role for civil society and local communities in the administration of land. This report critically examines the framework of these approaches in the light of a comparative case study located in two areas of southern Ghana. It argues that rural areas are undergoing considerable transformation at present under liberalisation and it examines the implications of this fluidity for the conception of the role of the "community" in land administration.

Evolutionary Property Rights School

The evolutionary property rights school has been highly influential in defining the World Bank's position on land reform, particularly as stated in the Bank's 1975 Land Tenure Policy Reform Programme. The document presents an ideal vision of what land reform should strive to attain.

The ideal unit of agricultural production is seen as the owner-operated family farm. This property-owning family unit is not socially defined, but it is clear that the evolutionary property rights school very much see this family in the image of the ideal American Judo-Christian conception of family. This is a nuclear two parent family, with children who help their parents on the farm with the aspiration of taking over the family farm from their ageing parents one day (Deininger and Bisnwanger, 1998). The problems of defining families, households, units of production, consumption and reproduction, one parent families, matrilineal conceptions of kin, and extended networks of kin are not considered. The farm unit is also not defined and it is presumed that the family farm consists of one contiguous unit which is passed down from parents (probably the assumption is the father) to children (probably thought of as sons). The concept of a farmer working on several different plots that were acquired in different ways from different people does not feature in this conception of farm.

The evolutionary property rights school argue that the 'family farm' is the most efficient unit of agricultural production and the most equitable. Family farms are seen as more efficient since family members are residual claimants to profits and thus have higher incentives to provide effort than hired labour. They share in the risk of production and lower the transaction costs—they can be employed without incurring hiring or search or supervisory costs (Brandão and Feder, 1995).

The main concern with tenure reform in this framework is with promoting forms of secure, private ownership for the agrarian nuclear family and a free market in land. The emergence of private land markets is seen as promoting the transfer of land to more efficient users and equity in which family farms can purchase more land when they need it and sell off surplus land. Secure and enforceable property rights are seen as a precondition for investment and economic growth. The development of a land market enables farmers to access credit markets through land as collateral, to gain risk insurance, and to smooth consumption by selling land (Carter and Zimmerman, 1993).

According to the evolutionary property rights school the emergence of credit markets enables farmers to gain access to loans to purchase new technologies for farm improvement and increased production. Increased population density requires that farmers substitute land fallowing technologies with fertility-restoring technologies. This requires farmers to change their practice and invest in new technologies and make a long-term commitment to farm investment. This commitment to investment requires that farmers have security of land ownership and confidence to put capital into the land. Security and proof of land ownership give banks and financial services confidence to give loans to farmers against the collateral of the land.

Without access to credit and insurance, farmers develop inefficient and costly substitute strategies. They diversify production into low-risk low-return sectors as a cushion against unpredictable shocks and to ensure satisfaction of minimum subsistence requirements (Rosenzweig and Binswanger, 1993; Brandão and Feder, 1995; Feder and Feeny, 1991). Access to credit and insurance enables farmers to enter into high-risk high-return economic activities. It enables them to consume modern technologies developed by international agricultural research and agribusiness. Land reform is seen as being critical to the uptake of modern agricultural technology. Land titling is seen as the major avenue promoting land reform and security of land tenure, as enabling farmers to have access to collateral through which they can gain credit.

These premises remain at the heart of the World Bank's programme on land reform. However, in line with the recent structural adjustment programme, economic liberalisation approaches and reflections on experiences since the 1970s in implementing land reform these positions have been reappraised. Current land policy thinking is concerned with conceptualising land reform within a framework of institutional reform in which civil society plays a greater role in the administration of land. This role will complement or replace the government role in setting up land titling and cadastre programmes. The involvement of civil society in land administration is seen as promoting greater efficiency, by creating institutions that can absorb the transaction costs of successful land administration or suppress the increasing transaction costs of poor state administration.

Feder and Feeny (1991) argue that property rights need to be placed within their institutional setting. They define three distinct types of institutional structure: constitutional, institutional and normative behaviour. The constitutional order consists of the major rules that define how society is organised—"the rules for making the rules" (Feder and Feeny, 1991). Institutional arrangements are laid down by the constitutional order and they consist of the laws, regulations, contracts, associations, and include property rights. The normative values consist of the cultural values which legitimise institutional arrangements and constrain behaviour. In the process of social and economic transformation these three orders of institutional structure may develop discordantly. While the formal institutional structure of land tenure may support private property through a formally established legal framework, the corresponding registration and enforcement mechanism may be absent. The normative values of the majority of farmers may be based on forms of customary tenure which are not recognised in law, or even made illegal (e.g. pledging of land). The institutional arrangements necessary for enforcement of property rights, including courts, police, financial institutions, land surveys, record keeping may not be in place, or may create expenses in land registration that the majority of farmers are unwilling to bear.

Unless appropriate institutional arrangements are created for the administration of land rights, disincentives will be created that will lead to land market distortions. Unless financial institutions and technology development options are in place which will enable increased security in land to be transformed into collateral, loans and modern technology, land titling can lead to speculation in land for rentier capital (Feder and Feeny, 1991).

With these factors in mind property rights analysts have tempered their original optimism in land titling as a mechanism of fostering land reform and access to credit for improved agricultural performance. They have developed a model of an evolutionary sequence of land rights. Private property is seen as evolving in response to increases in the scarcity value of land. Forms of private titling and the institutional infrastructure necessary for regulating land ownership develop when the benefits from precise and secure land rights become clear. When land is abundant and labour scarce, property rights in labour are of more concern than property rights in land. Under these circumstances people can be used as pledges rather than land. Within small communities land rights are often secure and transparent, since land is transferred according to established customary norms and communities can prevent outsiders from encroaching. With increasing commercialisation of agriculture and increasing scarcity of land, people move to frontier areas and new areas are opened up for cultivation. Land disputes become endemic and land acquires a scarcity value. Considerable costs are spent on disputes and litigation. Under these circumstances it becomes economic to introduce a comprehensive framework of land administration with record keeping, surveys and legal administration. This is further enhanced by the development of financial institutions, insurance institutions and modern technology which enable land to be used as collateral for access to technologies for production and insurance against risk. Titled land becomes highly valued and a land market develops according to the productive needs of farming units (Feder and Feeny, 1991).

This concept of evolutionary land markets supports a more demand-driven approach to land reform in which titling only becomes one option adopted in relation to the level of development of agricultural support services. Where conditions for the operation of formal titling programmes do not exist, community-based solutions can be devised (Bruce, 1993). Programmes can be developed which seek to strengthen community-based administration of land, strengthen definitions of rights in "communal tenure systems" and facilitate their further evolution into a private land market:

> Instead of recommending abandonment of communal tenure systems in favor of freehold title and subdivision of the commons (as in the LRPP), the Bank now recognizes that communal tenure systems are often a more cost-effective solution than formal title and that, in situations where this is the case, efforts to reduce the cost of cooperation, improve accountability, and facilitate evolution of communal systems in response to local needs may be needed (Deininger and Binswanger, 1998: Introduction, p. 2).

This new approach stresses that greater attention must be paid to the conditions under which titling is viable, since where credit markets are imperfect titling can favour richer and more influential sectors in society. Under these distortions land sales markets may neither increase efficiency or equity but lead to land speculation and expropriation of land to the disadvantage of small-scale producers. A more integrated approach to the development of rural factor markets is required. The focus is moving towards developing integrated and decentralised pilot projects in specific localities rather than supporting national land titling programmes (Deininger and Binswanger, 1998).

However, within this framework the underlying premises of the Land Tenure Reform Policy still remain intact. Individual land ownership and the emergence of a land market are seen as the ultimate objective of land tenure reform, and the ideal institutional forms promoting security of land, equity and economic efficiency. Various transitional programmes are supported to facilitate the evolution of individual land property and the owner-occupied family farm, and to support security of land ownership in the transition from communal land to private land. As Deininger and Binswanger (1998) comment:

Group titles that specify boundaries and thus limit encroachment by outsiders are a promising solution but more efforts are required to develop rules of accountability to guide administration of such rights within the community and to ensure a smooth and decentralized transition towards full private property rights at the appropriate moment.

Institutional arrangements: The communitarian approach

In contrast to the evolutionary school of land rights and its roots in neo-liberal economics, the communitarian approach to land tenure is influenced by anthropological, cultural studies and customary law approaches. The communitarian approach stresses that tenure relations are rooted in social relations and cultural beliefs. It holds that these relations do not fit into a pattern of evolutionary determinism and insists on the diversity of human societies and diversity of institutional solutions to social problems. It is concerned with *local* perceptions of land relations, and local norms and practices relating to land tenure, and the administration and regulation of land, customary practices and customary authority (Lavigne Delville, 1998). It challenges perspectives solely based on private ownership and economic efficiency and argues that land reform needs to meet the needs of rural communities and their socio-cultural value systems. Toulmin and Quan (2000:3) argue that land reform should:

> ... search for approaches that are practical, democratic and consistent with African socio-cultural values. In most African customary traditions, rights are established to land by birth, kinship, and investment of sweat and toil, as well as by social contract. In a continent where poverty, vulnerability and human suffering have been endemic in many regions, the approach to land policy and land rights needs to be strongly human-centred, and less driven by economic prescription than government and donors have frequently allowed. Land policy and land law need to be more even-handed in relation to the various stakeholders, particularly the poor. This requires a fundamental recognition that imported western notions of property rights are not the only principle which may be appropriate in Africa.

Communitarians reject the framework of the evolutionary property rights school, in which the objectives of land tenure reform are to create a land market that will enable farmers to gain loans for investment in improved agricultural technology. They are more concerned with the existing insecurity in land tenure arrangements. They argue that under customary arrangements land tenure can be secure and land administration can be effective. They see insecurity in land relations as a product of state-led policies and legal pluralism. Legal pluralism is a product of colonialism, in which colonial powers imposed their legal traditions on top of local land-holding systems. They attempted to interpret African tenure systems and codify them, but in the process the working of these systems was distorted by lenses fashioned by European perceptions of land at the end of the nineteenth century. Modern land law in Africa refers to legislation founded on colonial law at the beginning of the last century (Lavigne Delville, 2000).

Customary land tenure systems are not inherently unstable. Local land use rights and rules are frequently clearly understood within the communities in which they operate. However, they are often not legally recognised. The existence of legal pluralism creates confusion in which the rights to different areas of adjacent land may be established by different legal codes. This creates uncertainty in rights to land, since they can be challenged and cancelled through appeal to different state authorities. The confusion surrounding land rights benefits the politico-administrative class and their allies. They can take advantage of the confusion and use their influence to acquire land and control various forms of rents and bribes gained from the land (Lavigne Delville, 2000). Statutory frameworks governing relations between the state and the populace are often based on decisions that favour a particular group of people. They are based on specific political alliances (Lavigne Delville, 1998). Statutory frameworks are not neutral.

Communitarians are concerned with harmonising local practice and state administration in land. They seek to facilitate dialogue between different stakeholders to achieve a better integration of land policy and a more transparent land policy that meets the needs of various land-users and stakeholders.

Communitarians are also concerned with building local capacities to manage land and engage in dialogue. As Platteau (2000:72) comments:

> What is therefore needed is an approach based on cooperation rather than confrontation. This implies, whenever feasible, a strengthening of local capacities for management, information, and dispute settlement rather than imposing from above the mechanisms of a formal legal system. In most cases, it also implies recognising the rights of original occupants to "vacant" land located in their ancestral territory.

Problems in defining the community

The communitarian approach successfully challenges some myths that underlie the evolutionary property rights theory of land tenure. It challenges the ethnocentrism of evolutionary property rights theory and shows that property has other significance than a means of gaining loans to purchase modern agricultural technology. It argues that the significance of land should be determined by the various stakeholders to that land rather than by western notions of property, masquerading as objective, neutral, scientific or technocratic definitions. It shows that what is construed as a tenure system consists of different elements interacting in political space and that tenure systems are not solely evolving in relationship to systemic factors of population, land scarcity and technological development. Political factors have an important influence on tenure systems. The communitarian approach demonstrates that what is construed as evolution towards higher individuated tenure systems often consists of a struggle between customary forms of land tenure and legal forms of private property which the state attempts to impose. Far from being modern, these state forms of land tenure are based on colonial models of tenure which were imposed at the beginning of colonial rule and which do not reflect the realities of contemporary rural Africa. Customary forms of land tenure are seen as dynamic with the capacity to respond to changing conditions.

Arcadian Africa and authentic culture

In counterposing the state to the customary world, the communitarians fall back on an inverted dualism which mirrors that used in modernisation theory, between the traditional and modern sector. It is inverted in the sense that while economic dualism portrayed the traditional sector as backward and the modern sector as progressive, the traditional or customary sector is now being characterised as dynamic.

For many communitarianists this dualism does not constitute a problem. They are happy to fall back on the image of an Arcadian African tradition rooted in a deeply egalitarian moral order in which to portray the customary against a modern corrupt and inequitable state. A typical example of this Arcadian position is stated by Okoth-Ogendo (1994: 23–24):

> In former days, indigenous land use communities recognized the harshness of the environment and sought to cope with it through a number of institutional structures, principles and techniques. Over time these communities also devised ways of addressing the population issue, especially as it approached critical dimensions in particular localities.
>
> … The purpose of vesting the control function in the political authority of the community—the head of the family, the common ancestor or a council of elders—was generally three-fold. First and foremost, it was meant to guarantee security of opportunity for all who had access rights to those resources. If there were a possibility that some of these rights would be taken away, the tenure system assured that these would occur only in exceptional circumstances, and only upon a collective decision made at the highest level of social organization. Second, it was designed to ensure equity between and across generations. Thus the control function determined the rate of expansion or contraction of membership in the unit by means other than birth, and the distribution or redistribution of access rights in response, *inter alia*, to increased demand for land. Third, the control function also determined important land use decisions, such as specific land usages in particular areas of community territory, including planting, weeding and harvesting times, the duration of fallow periods, and the nature of resource preservation or conservation measures, where these required collective action by the community.

Communitarians often contrast this moral, egalitarian Arcadian tradition with a corrupt and inequitable modern state. For instance, Kasanga (1996:100) argues that the postcolonial land machinery in Ghana has been "inequitable , unjust, callous, inefficient, wasteful, and hopelessly corrupt". This is contrasted with the essence of customary tenure:

> Ghanaian customary tenurial systems are therefore a source of social security and continuity. The full enjoyment of the fruits of one's labour and efforts are guaranteed, and in regard to land, no man is "big" or "small" in his own village or town (Kasanga, 1996 :89).

He advocates that the chiefs and landowners rather than decentralised district authorities should be made responsible for land administration and that they should run their own autonomous land offices independently of the elected district assemblies.[1]

Other communitarians are troubled by this Arcadian perspective. As Lavigne Delville (2000:114–115) states:

> ... to recognise the existence and legitimacy of rights is not the same as going back to some idealised notion of "traditional" systems. The local context in Africa has changed; landholding practices and rights to land have progressed. The existing reality, with all its complexity and hybrid forms, must be taken as the starting point, rather than taking a neo-traditionalist stance and advocating "customary" rules which are no longer enforced, or simply allowing customary authorities complete control.

Lavigne Delville (2000:98–99) attempts to overcome the Arcadian position by unravelling underlying principles that inform the evolution and diversity of African land tenure systems:

> The distribution of rights is, therefore, based on the socio-political system (the political history of the village and region from which the alliances and hierarchical relationships between lineage are derived) and on family relations (access to land and resources depending on one's social status within the family), so that social networks govern access rights (Berry, 1993). Far from being the result of a series of precise rules, rights held by individuals are the fruits of negotiation in which the local land authorities act as arbiters; customary law is by nature "procedural" and not codified. It does not define each person's right, but the procedures by which access to resources is obtained.

> These basic principles continue to apply in most of rural Africa, even though the authorities, socio-economic conditions and the rights themselves have profoundly changed over time.... As is demonstrated by many case studies,

---

[1] This returns to the state of colonial administration under indirect rule, preceding reforms in the 1950s that introduced elected local councils.

local landholding systems do not consist of the rigid rights so often prescribed in earlier academic literature. They are flexible, and evolve in accordance with customary practice whereby rights are negotiated with the authorities on the basis of a number of shared principles.... Tenure rules often evolve in the face of major changes in the condition of production, or when the pressure on resources increases. There is no system that is "traditional" or customary in itself, but there are forms of land management based on customary principles.

There are also some problems with this schema. Firstly, it is not clear whether the underlying customary principles are projected as emic principles discovered by the researchers or etic principles, recognised as core values of authentic African culture on which they construct their tenure systems. Since no evidence is provided of their conscious articulation in African societies as principles they would appear to be emic categories. Secondly there is some confusion as to whether they are cultural principles confined to and characterising African societies or common underlying structural principles of accommodation and consensus-forming that are common to all societies. If these are emic principles of a more structural nature then there is a possibility that they are being imposed upon African societies by European researchers. The authentic African culture that is projected by these researchers is based on value systems that harmonise with the present niche role that Western politicians, policymakers and some Africanists have taken on as facilitators of peace and development, and as facilitators of dialogue between the state and civil society. In this respect they may be no more objective statements than colonial interpretations of African land tenure systems. If colonialist land theorists required rigid concepts of customary land law welded to tradition and traditional authority in which to construct their codification of customary land law, then present day facilitators require concepts of flexible land law which establish rights through a process of negotiation.

This tinkering with cultural values becomes most evident when community values conflict with global protocol. For instance, when dealing with issues of the environment, Dubois (1997) extols the virtues of the *Dina* in Madagascar as a model example of a customary institution that can be used for the modern regulation of natural resources. *Dina* are bye-laws enacted by traditional authorities, infringement of which includes fines, ritual sacrifices and expulsion from the community. That these may conflict with the human rights of peasant cultivators does not bother Dubois. However, when it comes to issues of *gender*, then he is concerned that customary institutions do not often promote women's interests and may need to be modified. Similarly, Egbe (1996) advocates the preservation of customary practices that are in accord with modern global environmental sensibilities and the modification of those which are at variance with global environmentalism:

This is not a wholesale justification of customary practices, but an argument
for perspective and balance. Slash-and-burn agriculture, shifting cultivation,
hunting with the use of fire and poisonous substances, and the rule that "he
who chops down the forest first establishes title", are certainly factors which
render customary practices invalid in terms of possible legislation. ... In ethnic
groups with a pyramidal power structure, such as most of the *lamidos* of the
Northern provinces, peasants are discouraged from planting trees because
they enjoy only usufruct. Consequently, they cannot develop the land on a
permanent basis. Efforts should be geared towards encouraging the aban-
donment, or at least modification of such practices. But a practice by which
certain animals enjoy royal status and therefore cannot be killed or hunted
could be beneficial for sustainable management. In the centralised system of
the West and North West Provinces, because the chiefs are the tutelar owner
of all land, their authority is respected in all matters pertaining to the land.
Sustainable management and conservation can be encouraged through such
centralised authorities (1996:31–32).

The depiction of an authentic African culture built on core values of processes of negotiation, accommodation and consensus-building, does not
easily fit with what we know of the history of Africa, particularly the large
number of wars between competing states and revolutionary upheavals
within societies that occurred in the nineteenth century. For instance in
writing on the development of militant Islam in West Africa, Levtzion
(2000:85) comments:

> It is significant that all leaders of jihad movements in West Africa came from
> the countryside and not from commercial or capital towns. The challenge to
> the marginal role of Islam in African society could not have come from those
> who had benefited from the existing political order—neither from traders
> who were protected from by the rulers nor from clerics who rendered relig-
> ious services in the chiefly courts.

> The new Muslim leaders articulated the grievances of peasants. In Hausaland
> 'Uthman Dan Fodio criticized the rulers for killing people, violating their
> honour, and devouring their wealth. He declared that "to make war on the
> oppressor is obligatory by assent". 'Uthman's son, the sultan Muhammad
> Bello, evoked the wrath of Allah over "the *amir* (ruler) who draws his suste-
> nance from the people but does not bother to treat them justly".

In this account of radical upheaval carried out under the inspiration of militant Islam, the rulers who were overthrown by an aggrieved rural society
are perceived in very much the same way as communitarians today perceive
contemporary states. But, the rural peasantry embrace radical Islam as an
ideology that would redress the injustices of their world, including rulers
who oppress and marginalise them. The peasantry do not resort to a doctrine of authentic African egalitarian values, which are being violated by
bad rulers and policymakers. The existing political system is seen as corrupt
and exploitative, in need of radical transformation through a reorganisation

of the political and social institutions and structures that existed in the nineteenth century.

Social differentiation and control over land

The issue of social differentiation is not easily dealt with by communitarians in their search for an authentic African democratic tradition which mirrors contemporary global morality. This issue is either avoided or sidestepped. Platteau (2000:72), for instance, skirts the issue of social differentiation, but then dogmatically asserts African communal values:

> ... even though social differentiation is not to be underestimated, African village communities tend to provide social security to all their members and to ensure that everybody can participate in new opportunities. Such considerations of social security and equity usually dominate pure efficiency concerns, which should be regarded as a positive contribution in a generally insecure economic environment. Third, even today, customary systems continue to generate a remarkable degree of consensus, in particular on the norms and values justifying land claims.

Perhaps, an issue of more fundamental concern is that communitarians deal with social institutions but not the social alignments around these institutions. They do not pay sufficient attention to the relations between social classes or social interest groups around which institutions are organised. They do not go beyond the social sensibilities of global protocol, which require gender, street children, and various "minority" groups to be considered, or beyond the concept of a stakeholder. These liberal social concepts are imposed on the societies in question rather than arising from a social analysis of the social relations around production and market exchange. Stakeholders are conceived of as autonomous interest groups with an interest in a resource, which they come to negotiate with other users around a negotiating table. Stakeholders are not usually conceived of as locked into pre-existing socioeconomic relations with each other.

A number of researchers have highlighted the relationship between political struggles to define and redefine social relations and rights in land. These relationships and struggles are transformed by changes in the conditions of production and different historical circumstances. For instance, Parkin (1972) argues that the main avenue of social differentiation among Giriama in Kenya is the acquisition of land for cultivation of coconut palms. Entrepreneurial farmers are investing in land and palms. The Giriama are an egalitarian society in which wealth in the past has been expressed by attracting and maintaining supporters, rather than by investing in land. To create a land market the entrepreneurial farmers manipulate bridewealth and funeral expenses to gain access to land. Through increasing ostentation the costs of hosting these two occasions are increased and many families are forced to sell land to raise finances. These enterprising farmers maintain a network of influential elders who act as informants on available land for sale and as witnesses to land transactions. Since land sales are not registered it is important for the purchasers of the land to have elders as witnesses. Government courts also regard the testimonies of elders more favourably than other members of the community. The enterprising farmers continue to subscribe to the "common language of custom" playing important roles in customary institutions and upholding the authority of elders and lineage heads. By acting as witnesses in land transactions the authority of elders is upheld, but the elders also sanction the rights of young farmers to buy land and gain access to land without reference to kinship relations (on which the authority of the gerontocrats is ultimately based). The elders attach themselves as clients to young wealthy farmers. Through their role as witnesses the elders uphold the gerontocratic ideal and yet subscribe to the capitalist spirit which threatens to undermine the ideal of age as the prerequisite of authority. The enterprising farmers support the ideals of redistribution and the principle of seniority, but conceal illicit capitalist principles under the cloak of gerontocratic authority. Parkin refers to the process as the "mystification of social inequality".

In the Murang'a district of Kenya, MacKenzie (1993) shows how Kikuyu men seek to gain control over land claimed by women by manipulating the tradition of *mbari* or patrilineal sub-clan authority. She argues that this recourse to "traditional" lineage structures is used to mask an ongoing process of socioeconomic differentiation. This has eroded women's individual rights in land. However, women have responded by manipulating other social idioms to organise for their rights, and developed other idioms which combine modern organisation with appeal to tradition. MacKenzie argues that both the customary and statutory spheres are arenas for the struggles of men and women for land.

In a study of conflicts over irrigated rice lands in the Gambia, Watts (1993), focuses on household gender conflicts over access to land and labour. Men attempt to gain control over land and crop rights in the irrigation project by classifying the newly created plots as household plots on which all household members must work. Under this arrangement women find themselves losing the individual plots they used to farm as they become incorporated into irrigation land and reclassified as household plots. Women have resisted these developments by withdrawing their labour from these plots and challenging their classification as household plots. Property rights are thus defined by evolving social relations, including gender roles and labour arrangements. Watts (1993:161–162) argues that:

> ... property rights must not be seen as narrowly material for they represent rights with respect to people, including rights over their labour power. Rights over resources such as land or crops are inseparable from, indeed are isomorphic with, rights over people; to alter rights is , as Robert Bates says, to rede-

fine social relationships. And second, by seeing economic life as a realm of representations, we perceive struggles over land and labor to be simultaneously symbolic contests and struggles over meaning. In the case I examine, specifically, who works where under what conditions, and the conjugal contract. In conditions in which households are contracted on as the basic unit of production, the consequences for the labor process (the social organization of work) and property are always domestic in character, reflecting the dominance of kinship and gender in the access to, and control over, resources.

On the basis of such detailed case studies, the dichotomy between a state which promotes capitalist spirit and land grabbing by its allies and a community committed to egalitarian social values and social welfare principles is difficult to substantiate. The capitalist spirit eats deep into communities and becomes internalised in its social institutions and representations of custom and culture.

In a study of the Guro, Meillassoux (1978) argues that the incorporation into the world market economy was accompanied by a transformation of the expropriation of the land. This resulted in a relaxation of kinship relations that had become incompatible with the relations of production that emerged from the "valorisation of the product of labour" (1978:327). Land became the object of contract between owners and tenants, employers and labourers that replaced earlier relations of personal dependence. Meillassoux argues that peasant society is transformed, but its traditional sector features continue to be retained because it continues to have value to international capitalism, in providing the social welfare functions and basic needs which capitalism refuses to assume. Thus, the persistence of customary institutions is less dependent upon their innate "conservatism", "adaptability" or "flexibility" than on the continued interest of international capitalism in perpetuating these forms. Meillassoux (1978:328) concludes that:

> [In Guro society] community organisation is already in the process of disintegrating through the spread of trade, the commercialisation of food products and agricultural specialisation. Around cash crops there tends to develop a fragmented peasantry still rooted in former structures and representations which conceal the emergence of a new class of landowners. But the new peasantry will be able to recognise the true nature of the new social relations, as the wage-earners push the young villagers away to the city, as the competing immigrant planters ruin local farmers and as big private owners expropriate the village community.

Community boundaries and community representation

Without a concept of a wider social structure in which communities are integrated the boundaries and social representation of communities are difficult to define. The concept of community comes to define the institutions in which the peasantry live, the institutions within a settlement. But these institutions are not placed within a social structure in which they operate. They are not placed within polities or other social and political structures and the hierarchies of settlement which come to define polities.

This leads to much confusion in the identification of rights of representation between different groups. As we have seen above, Platteau (2000:72) defines community representation in terms of "recognising the rights of original occupants to "vacant" land. Lavigne Delville (2000:118), on the other hand, recognises the danger of this position:

> Claims based on "prior occupancy" or "indigenous occupancy" are particularly problematic. While they are an issue for legitimisation, they are often the basis used to justify the revival of "ancestral" rights that may have been lost, or to challenge open-ended loans of land that have, over time, been transformed into de facto ownership. In some cases, the intervention of the Rural Land Plan in Ivory Coast has enabled local people to claim ownership of land that has been made available to a group of incomers several generations ago.

It is not clear how contested rights between different groups, who may use different idioms of custom to represent their interests or alternative discourses can be dealt with within this framework of community consensus.

Problems of representation very much influenced the dismembering of Indirect Rule in British colonies, during the 1950s. It was realised that the rapid social change and migrations that had accompanied the economic developments of staple crop farming and extractive industry resulted in a social flux. The heterogeneous populations of villages, towns and districts reflected a situation of cultural pluralism rather than conformity to a single customary code. The imposition of conceptions of native administration based on a concept of tribal chiefs resulted in much discontent. This realisation resulted in reforms to develop local administration in the 1950s based on elected councils.

The major focus of communitarians is on totalizing discourses centred on strong social relations with a clearly defined political structure that represents the community. These institutions share a common culture with an underlying system of shared values to which all actions and discourses are connected. While history is not denied, it is seen as a vehicle through which these underlying values are recognised. While conflicts and contestation of resources are not denied they are attributed to be a characteristic of this underlying authentic culture.

The communitarian approach recognises patterns of inequality at the national level between the state and the locality, but is weak in analysing social differentiation within the rural or community structure. This is not surprising since it centres its analysis on authority structures. It fails to develop a framework through which processes of contestation, transformation and domination can be analysed (Asad, 1979), in which a variety of discourses can develop around land including potentially subversive positions.

Change and transformation

By defining the customary as flexible, adaptive, dynamic and hybrid, the communitarian approach creates problems for examining processes of change, since change has now become an intrinsic feature of institutions rather than a product of struggle between different social forces. While the communitarian approach paints African cultures in a positive way, the concept of adaptive social-welfare oriented communities may not actually correspond with the realities of living at the turn of the century. Some recent research has suggested that the last twenty years of readjustment policies following on from recession have resulted in a "declining coherence of peasantries, with respect to their marketable farm production, family structures, class position and rural communities" (Bryceson, 2000).

Diminishing incomes from cash crops have undermined the position of men as family providers. Many children and youths have been forced to become involved in income-generating activities outside of family farm labour and outside of the agricultural sector. This has resulted in a new individualisation of economic activity which undermines family labour and the pooling of resources, as members of families begin to assert their economic independence. There is an increasing mobility with large numbers of people moving between rural towns and villages and between urban and rural areas. Many rural households are involved in non-agricultural activities and agricultural incomes are often supplemented with non-farm work. There is increasing social differentiation. Family networks and reciprocal relations are increasingly becoming ambiguous as family units are being transformed (Bryceson, 2000). Structurally, there is an outflow of capital and labour from agriculture towards service sector oriented economic activities.

Tensions within the units of rural production, consumption and distribution have been exacerbated by adjustment policies. Under these policies communities have become responsible for raising funds for their own development and supporting their own social safety networks to see to their welfare, for bearing the transaction costs of development. While this is heralded by new institutional economists as a radically new path-breaking theory, this is an old theory, which lay at the heart of colonial Indirect Rule, of "government on a shoestring". Behind the attempt of communitarians to build a new participatory local-level democracy, based on notions of redistributional community institutions with responsibility for social welfare and arbitration of disputes, lies this concept of communities bearing the transaction costs of development. If community social welfare and redistributional institutions are being rapidly transformed under the pressure of increasing hardship, immiseration, social differentiation, and as a result of the new roles ascribed for them by international development policy, then the foundations of present policy will be badly informed. Without subjecting notions of African society and popular participation to careful scrutiny, social scien-

tists and development theorists run the risk of developing vicarious para-
digms with unforeseen consequences. As Parkin (1972:104) concludes in his
study of changing Giriama land relations:

> Insofar as we follow unquestioning many customs and conventions in our
> own particular culture, we are all mystified into accepting certain assump-
> tions about our place in society and about human existence generally. Yet at
> the same time we remain unaware of the long-term implications of our values
> and beliefs.

An outline of what lies ahead

This work examines property relations in the Akyem Abuakwa area of the
forest region of Ghana. The Akyem Abuakwa area is the old cocoa frontier
zone in Ghana in which migrant cocoa farmers started purchasing lands
during the nineteenth century. It is an area rich in agricultural land and gold
and diamonds. The study focuses on two areas: the Atewa Range and the
New Suhum area. In all three settlements the dominant kinship organisation
is matrilineal—although in the Suhum area a large proportion of the
migrants are not matrilineal. The main crop in the New Suhum settlement is
cocoa. Cocoa production has declined in the Atewa Range settlements. Experiencing difficulty in rehabilitating cocoa, roots and tubers have become
the main farm produce. The main cash crop is plantain.

Two adjacent citizen Akyem communities are examined in the Atewa
Range, where communities are hemmed in by a forest reserve and suffer
some consequences of land shortage resulting from this appropriation of
land by the colonial state. Social differentiations in landholdings are not so
pronounced in this area and the main differentiation takes place across
generations. The grandparent generation has the most access to land by
virtue of establishing ownership through land clearance in the pioneer frontier days of cocoa cultivation. The youth suffer the most from land shortage,
and become dependent upon their families for land. Unlike in the past, they
no longer have the option of going out and clearing their own patch of forest, because uncultivated forests, outside of the forest reserve, no longer
exist. However, the male youth also find family dependency constraining
and no longer wish to serve their fathers and uncles on the farm. This is
partly because their elders cannot support them materially and meet their
basic needs in an increasingly expensive world. Elders cannot guarantee
them access to land at the end of their service, since land has become scarce
in relation to the number of people with rights in land. Family disputes may
develop around elders giving out land or leaving land as an inheritance to
their children or sisters' children. As a result of tensions between male
youth, fathers and mothers' brothers over rights to land and rights to labour
service, many male youth attempt to get land from other sources, appealing
to grandparents who have more land than their parents (and fewer desires),

or entering into contractual sharecrop arrangements with farmers outside their families. Others gain their income by hiring themselves out as casual labourers to other farmers, engage in goldmining, diamond mining, and carry timber boards for chainsaw operators (many of whom operate illegally). Many young people migrate to towns and cities and other villages, all in search of work.

As a result of these livelihood strategies of youth, their seniors no longer have access to family labour and have to hire labour. Those that cannot afford the cost of hiring labour or are unwilling to supervise labour, engage in sharecrop contracts with "youth" tenants. Elders are also selling land. This is sold under the cloak of family distress, but frequently this is a deliberate strategy to destroy family property and recreate land as individual property. By developing a land market elders can transform family land into individual land. They may use some of the proceeds gained from sales of family land to purchase their own individual land. In contrast to family property, they can use individual property as they wish and are free to disburse it as they please. At the level of land sales the interests of youth and elders may coincide. The development of a land market enables youth with money to purchase their own land and farm independently. It enables fathers to pass on land to their children without other family members contesting this process. While land can be purchased easily, purchases are limited because of lack of capital within the area and the lack of a prosperous agricultural base.

Land relations and disputes also have a gender dimension. Many women are concerned that men are attempting to pass on land to their own sons at the expense of their daughters. Women are defining their rights in land according to a new interpretation of matrilineal inheritance which attempts to exclude men such as brothers, nephews and uncles from matrilineal land. They argue that if land is passed on to male heirs the men will give portions of the matrilineal land to their wives and children, thus diminishing the land the matrilineage has at its disposal. In contrast, if the land goes to the women of the lineage, their husbands will help them to develop the land, but it will be inherited by children who are of the matrilineage, thus consolidating matrilineal property. This ideology promotes the role of women as custodians of the matrilineage. In contrast with many contemporary approaches to gender equality which seek to strengthen the rights of wives and children to the property of men, this discourse prefers to strengthen women's direct rights in matrilineal land. Land is seen as an asset through which a woman can gain a good hardworking husband and retain rights in land. This is seen as preferable to the situation where a wife serves her husband and gains secure rights in his property. This reflects a situation where marriage is frequently unstable. While this discourse is articulated to appeal to matrilineal sentiments and custom, it essentially subverts matrilineal authority by questioning the allegiance of the male head of the matrilineage to matrilineal principles. It takes advantage of attempts of males to shift the burden of their responsibility towards their sisters' children and the rift between male elders and male youth, to redefine matriliny according to matrifocal principles, based on the unity of three generations of female relatives.

The Aburi section of Kofi Pare in the New Suhum area also has a matrilineal ideology. However, there are significant differences in the way land is organised around this matrilineal ideology to the Atewa Range settlements. The Kofi Pare land was purchased in the late nineteenth century by wealthy farmer traders, who had accumulated capital in oil palm farming. A small group of wealthy male associates purchased a large tract of land jointly. They divided the land according to their contribution and then invited relatives to join them in their farming enterprise. The family members were given small plots of land on which to make their farms and provided labour service to their patrons for developing their large plantations and the settlement infrastructure. The wealthy patrons also brought labourers to the settlement. Some of these were rewarded with gifts of portions of land. As the settlement developed migrant labourers also gravitated towards the settlement. The large farmers released land to them on sharecropping arrangements. The large farmers had many farming ventures in different areas and managed these plantations by placing family members as caretakers and labourers in different localities and supplemented their labour with hired labour and sharecroppers. The various settlements in which they farmed developed a mosaic of social relations based on social differentiation, large holdings surrounded by small holdings and various forms of labourers, labour tenants and tenant farmers. Social differentiation within agriculture has a deeper history than in the Atewa Range settlements. Sharecropping arrangements are more deeply entrenched here, and are less generationally bound than in the Atewa Range settlements. Many latter day migrants moved to Kofi Pare in search of employment as labourers or as sharecrop tenants. However, similar tensions between youth and elders exist and are generated by the macroeconomic contexts. Youth are insecure about their future access to family land, are unwilling to spend long years in service to their elders for promises of land in the distant future, and are unsatisfied with the material support they gain from their elders. They seek to gain sharecropping land and develop alternative livelihood strategies to farming. Large numbers of youth migrate to towns and cities. The elders are unable to look after a large number of dependants and can no longer control the youth through demands of labour service. They attempt to limit their own family responsibility to their children and depend more upon sharecrop contracts than on hired labour. Thus, the same crisis of redistribution of land and labour, and increasing commodification of these relations occurs, as in the Atewa Range. Again, this is represented as an intergenerational conflict and as a moral crisis. The elders portray youth as lazy and disrespectful and the youth depict the elders as greedy and exploitative.

Most residents at Kofi Pare are adamant that a land market does not exist, since the land is family land, having being portioned out by matrilineal benefactors. However, more land sales occur at Kofi Pare than in the Atewa Range settlements, although they are kept very discreet. This probably reflects a higher demand for land than in the Atewa Range, given the greater wealth generated by cocoa than plantain. By maintaining a discreet sphere of land sales related to distress, land prices are maintained at a high level since land purchasers have to expend considerable resources in gaining information on available land. This assures that sharecrop tenants are not able to easily move from the economic sphere of dependent tenants to independent landowners, and that dependent youth cannot usurp their elders by purchasing land.

In contrast to the Atewa Range settlements, a matrifocal discourse is absent. Women exert little control over land and have very limited access to land. The position of most women in the settlement is defined by their relationship to men rather than to land. Many women define themselves as wives rather than farmers. This results from the origins of the settlement. A group of male associates came together to purchase land. They disbursed land to matrilineal supporters who helped them open the land and built up a following of labourers. The service and labour relations were relations between men. The role of women was in placing the men in matrilineages and maintaining the consumption and reproductive units of the men. The wealthy male farmer traders, cemented their economic partnerships by engaging in marriage alliances, which assured that their properties would be consolidated by their descendants. While they did apportion some land to female relatives, this was essentially for the benefit of their male children. Most women went to these frontier towns as wives of cocoa farmers. They were able to farm food crops on land their husbands were developing as cocoa plantations. As time went on the area of mature plantation expanded and the area of new plantation in which they could plant food crops diminished. Women's roles as farmers became increasingly marginalised.

Contemporary land relations cannot be analysed against a backdrop of customary relations, for what we construe to be customary relations have been developed in specific and changing historical relations. The customary setting of matrilineal land relations in Kofi Pare is different from those in the Atewa Range, because they reflect quite different historical processes. The original farmers at Kofi Pare, were wealthy pioneer frontier farmers, who created the cocoa economy of Ghana. The farmers in the Atewa Range who went out to create cocoa farms in the forests surrounding their settlements, were smallholder farmers, imitating the efforts of the large cocoa investors in a small way, to gain a little wealth from cocoa. Each of these categories reproduced the culture, organisational forms and material wealth that had been bequeathed to them by organisations rooted in family structures organised around three generations of sibling groups emanating from a grand old lady, in different ways.

Land relations need to be understood in terms of their historical roots in economic and material conditions, and how they are perceived and organised in terms of popular perceptions of those material conditions and the relation to the past. Every epoch produces its interpretation of the past and the present, of custom and modernity, of progress and transformation.

With this in mind, this first chapter of this study develops a historical overview of the Akyem area, and the changing significance of land, labour, polity and lineage in this changing political economy. The second chapter builds up a description of the three settlements that are the subject of the research and their economy. The third chapter examines the kinship relations between elders, youth, men and women in agricultural production, and how these relations are mediated by concepts of rights in land and labour, rights to service and welfare, and the commodification of land and labour. The final chapter examines the implications of these findings for present interpretations of the land question and the relevance of a land policy for rural development.

Chapter 1
The Setting

In Akyem Abuakwa as in Africa the management of land is rooted in religious and sacred beliefs. Most tribes share a common reverence for land as the foundation of community existence. The earth was regarded as a sanctuary of the souls of the departed ancestors who commanded the living to use the land wisely. As Nana Ofori Atta, the paramount chief of Akyem Abuakwa (or is it the Elusi of Odogbolu?)[2] said "land belongs to a vast family of whom many are dead, a few are living and countless hosts are still unborn". Land was the sanctuary of the departed souls of the ancestors and they commanded the living to use the land wisely. The living, particularly their chiefs and earth priests are the custodians of the land. A well known Akan proverb states: "The farm is mine but the soil belongs to the stool". Land is vested in the chief to manage on behalf of the community. Thus the allodial rights to land are vested in paramount stools (seats of power) who hold the land on behalf of the whole community and delegate them to subchiefs and lineages who help the customary trustees in all aspects of land management. The customary trustees fully recognise the birth rights and interests held by the individual citizens of the realm and the communal property rights of the community. The vesting of authority in chiefs assured equal access of all those with rights to land and ensured that the use of land is regulated to ensure its conservation and sustainable use. The reverence for land built into customary land systems ensures security of tenure for individuals, families and communities.

This chapter could have begun in this fashion. Such an introduction would have been in accord with mainstream received wisdom. Unfortunately, it does not sit very comfortably with a consideration of the history of Akyem Abuakwa and its bearing on land relations. Like most histories, that of Akyem Abuakwa is complex and multidimensional. It is messy and bound up with the quest for power and hegemony and also with struggles against oppression and injustice. Thus, this chapter examines the various dimensions of the land question by looking at the history of Akyem Abuakwa and its bearing on the way we conceive of land.

At the turn of the century Akyem Abuakwa was a major frontier zone of economic prosperity in the Gold Coast. It was rich in natural resources, in gold, diamonds, and timber. It was blessed with large areas of uncultivated

---

[2] Ollenu (1962) attributes this quote to Nana Ofori Atta I and Meek (1912) attributes it to the Elusi of Odogbolu. See Amankwah (1989:8).

Figure 1. *Akyem Abuakwa*

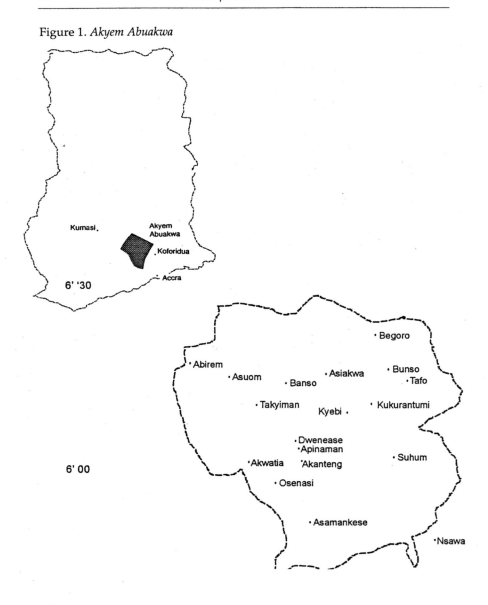

moist forest soils. Cocoa farmers thronged to Akyem Abuakwa from the old
export oil palm farming areas in Krobo and Akuapem, and concession
mongers purchased concessions from the chiefs. In this situation the
Okyenhene, the paramount chief of Akyem Abuakwa, Sir Nana Ofori Atta I,
attempted to establish control over the land of Akyem Abuakwa, to gain
access to valuable economic rents, and to prevent other chiefs becoming
more powerful than himself. In this process, he formed a close alliance with
the British colonialists and wholeheartedly embraced the concept of Indirect
Rule. In his desire to establish hegemony over a rapidly transforming
Akyem Abuakwa, he constructed a vision of a modern state built of an
authentic tradition, rooted in the conquest of the lands of Akyem Abuakwa
by the Ofori Panyin dynasty, and rights to overlordship and revenues from
the land acquired by the successors of Ofori Panyin from this historic event.
This conception of authentic tradition was contested by different sections of
people that made up the population of Akyem Abuakwa and by the 1940s
and 1950s this edifice crumbled as it became evident that the structure of
native authority administration was unworkable in what was a modern
plural society (Rathbone, 1996). Social and economic relations were being
governed by commodity production which was a far cry from the political
construction of an ethnic polity based on allegiance to a pure Akyem aristocracy. This chapter traces the conflicts and contradictions that have
emerged historically between the political conception of an authentic ethnic
based polity rooted in tradition and culture and the development of a modern economy producing for export markets.

The emergence of Akyem Abuakwa

The painstaking research of the historians Wilks (1977; 1982; 1993) and Kea
(1982) enables us to build up a picture of state formation in the Akan forest
areas. During the fourteenth century powerful and wealthy men began to
open up the forest region for gold extraction and agricultural production
with large numbers of retainers who were used for forest clearance. Having
opened up new areas for agricultural production the *abirempon* established
proprietary rights over the land, and exchanged usufructuary rights in land
and protection with migrating settler farmers for allegiance. Fierce competition developed for control over land and the organisations of *abirempon*
became militarised. Military service came to replace agricultural surplus
extraction as the mark of allegiance. Weaker *abirempon* became subordinate
to stronger ones and a hierarchy of allegiance grew from village chiefs
(*odikro*) to district chiefs the rulers of empires (*omanhene*). The state became
organised as a military formation in which the various subordinate settlements of a state were organised into several wings under generals (*asafoakye*
in Akyem).

As proprietors of land that they had opened up, the *abirempon* took a token part of the harvest at the Odwira festival, and a share of the natural resource wealth of the land, the game, snails, fish, kola and minerals. They could demand labour service of their subjects and military service and they could levy taxes for special purposes such as for military expenses (*peato*), funeral expenses (*ayito*) and for the costs of state functions (*omanto*). In addition they could raise revenues from hearing cases in their courts. Subordinate chiefs would render similar services to their overlords. The descendants of the proprietors became the *odehye*, the nobility. They were served by a large number of retainers, originating from unfree labour, who carried out administrative and economic functions, serving as their personal farmers, miners, household attendants and henchmen (Wilks, 1993: 91–126; Kea, 1983).

The mid-fifteenth to mid-seventeenth century was a period of intensive settlement expansion within the Pra Offin and Birim areas. These movements eventually gave rise to new states during the seventeenth century, in which Denkyira, Akwamu, Akyem, and Asante came into being. In the sixteenth century the dominant power in the present territory of Akyem Abuakwa was Akwamu, which controlled an empire extending from the present day Akyem states to areas east of the Volta river.

In the Pra-Offin basin an intense struggle for political hegemony emerged during the seventeenth century. These struggles were to lead to the formation of the Denkyira, Akyem and Asante empires. Akyem Abuakwa traditions record that their ancestors were settled in Adanse. They were members of the Asona *mmusua kesie* (clan) and had established a series of settlements including Adaboye, Akrokyere, Kokobiante and Sebenso. In the struggles of the seventeenth century these Asona towns were to come into conflict with the nascent Asante nation over land situated around the Oda river. The Asona clansmen fled from their Adanse homelands and moved south beyond the Pra river into territories bordering on Akwamu. They were accompanied by some Oyoko clansmen, who later on went to form settlements such as Begoro and Asiakwa (Addo-Fenning, 1997; Wilks, 1958).

During the eighteenth century, Akyem settlers began to move southwards towards the borders of Akwamu, engaging in skirmishes with the Akwamu and making incursions into their territory. In 1730, taking advantage of widespread discontent within the Akwamu empire, the Akyem supported the rebels based in the tributary provinces of Akwamu, in Accra, and what was to become the Akuapem area and defeated the Akwamu ruling class. Within the Akwamu heartlands there was considerable dissension and several towns remained neutral in the conflict including Asamankese. Following the defeat of the Akwamu, the Akwamu empire fell to the Akyem. While the Akyem had pretensions of becoming heir to the Akwamu empire, they were never able to achieve control over the tributary provinces of Akwamu, which began to exert their own independence, forming the constellation of states that exist today in the southeast—the Akuapem, the Dangme states, Accra, Anglo, etc (Wilks, 1958).

The defeat of Akwamu resulted in waves of Abuakwa migrants moving into the Birim area, into the Banso and Kwantanang area. These established independent settlements from the existing Akwamu settlements. The Akwamu heartlands, around the Atewa Range including settlements such as Asamankese, Akwatia, Boadua, Apapam, Kwaman, Otwereso, and Tafo to the Nyano hill area were placed under a defeated Akwamu general, Kwesi Biribi, to administer as an Akyem province. However, the Akyem were unable to exert control over this area and it became a largely lawless area from which remnants of Akwamu military bands attacked trading caravans and the surrounding people (Wilks, 1958). In 1738 the Abuakwa were still organising periodic punitive expeditions into the settlements of Old Akwamu. In 1742 the Akwamu settlements were placed under military surveillance in the light of an impending Asante attack (Wilks, 1958).

In 1742 the Akyem states were defeated by Asante and the rulers of Akyem Abuakwa and Akyem Kotoku were captured. Wilks (1958) suggests that one of the main reasons behind this attack was an Asante concern with keeping the trade routes to Accra open by subduing the old Akwamu. The Asante appointed a new Okyenhene and effected the move of the centre of the Akyem Abuakwa polity from Banso to Kyebi, from where they hoped to control the old Akwamu towns. Throughout the late eighteenth and early nineteenth century Akyem Abuakwa was torn by conflicts centred on support and opposition to Asante. In 1764 the Asante ransacked Kyebi and in 1772 Okyenhene Obirikorang was defeated by the Asante, forced out of his kingdom and replaced by an Asante selected Okyenhene, Twum Ampofo. In 1811 the Asante expelled Atta Wusu from his kingdom (Addo-Fening, 1997). However in 1826, Asante was forced to retreat from the south following its defeat at the battle of Akatamanso by an alliance of southern states with support from British and Danish forces. Akyem Abuakwa then became a part of the loose coalition of states under British protection, the Gold Coast Protectorate.

During the eighteenth and nineteenth centuries, there were considerable tensions between the various settlements and the Okyenhene in Akyem Abuakwa. In the early nineteenth century the Begorohene refused to surrender an elephant tusk seized from Asiakwa, which resulted in a war between Begoro and the Okyenhene, in which the Begoro and their Kamana subjects migrated to Gyakiti in present day Akwamu, and only returned under an Asante guarantee of protection against the Okyenhene (Addo-Fening, 1997). The Asiakwa similarly united with the Asante against the Okyenhene in the Asante invasion of 1811 (Addo-Fening, 1997). On the western border Akyem Abuakwa did not possess a clearly defined territorial border but rather a mosaic of towns and their land who owed allegiance to the Okyenhene, interspersed with towns owing allegiance to the other two Akyem states. Moreover several of these towns shifted their allegiance from time to time (Field, 1948). The Akyem Abuakwa state thus consisted of a core of Asona settlements with firm allegiance to the Okyenhene, surrounded by other settlements with doubtful allegiance, shifting allegiance and no allegiance. This included former Akwamu towns, some of which only became effectively incorporated into the Akyem state under Asante control of Akyem Abuakwa. Allegiances to the Okyenhene often crossed with other ties of affinity which linked some groups with Asante and others with Akwamu.

The origin of the Akyem Abuakwa reveals a state struggling to attain an identity in the turmoil and fluidity of the eighteenth and nineteenth centuries. It does not reveal a state with well established conventions and customs arising from the sanctity of a long tradition of dynastic rule. Major themes in the history of Akyem Abuakwa centre on migrations, the coming together of disparate groups, conflicts and wars of domination and against oppression. The history is essentially bound up with the failure of a political centre to exert and wield power as it would like and to fashion Abuakwa into a homogenous state in the image of the centre. Through the seizure of power various groups have tried to rewrite history and define tradition as they please, but the spirits of the past have eluded them, for the circumstances surrounding the creation of Abuakwa, the Akwamu of old, show that Abuakwa belongs to no one and to no one essentialist or authentic tradition.

New migrants and the commodification of land

A stream of migrants began to flow into the sparsely populated lands of Akyem Abuakwa in the nineteenth century. The first wave of migrants were Dwaben refugees, fleeing from Asante following civil war. These joined existing settlements and also established their own Dwaben settlements such as Enyiresi, Anweam, Asaman and Koforidua. They were welcomed by the Abuakwa and given land on which to settle, in the established tradition in which the enemy of my enemy is my friend, and in which refugees have rights to abode.

A second wave of migrants began to materialise around the 1840s. This consisted of Krobo and Akuapem (later to be joined by Anum) farmers in search of land to grow oil palms for the export trade. These farmers had exhausted their lands on the south-east forest fringe and sought to purchase land from the Akyem. The Krobo bought land in the direction of Begoro systematically extending the oil palm plantations they already possessed in the vicinity of the Volta. These land purchases had originally grown out of a process of forceful seizure of land from weaker neighbours. They were put under oil palms which were transported down the Volta to European markets. By the 1850s Krobo was producing about 60 percent of Gold Coast palm oil exports (Wolfson, 1953). With new-found wealth the Krobo sued for peace with their neighbours and offered to pay compensation for lands they had seized and to purchase any available lands. Vendors were found in the chiefs of the Begoro division, and the Krobo expanded deep into the forests (Amanor, 1994; Field, 1943; Johnson, 1964; 1965). Similarly, Akuapem farmers also began to purchase land beyond the Densu river in the New Suhum area.

This settlement of migrants in sparsely populated lands which Akyem Abuakwa had acquired through conquest did not create problems until the colonial period and the proclamation of the Native Jurisdiction Ordinance of 1883. As Addo-Fenning (1997) writes:

> Until 1883 the presence of migrant communities in Akyem Abuakwa created no serious political difficulties. The traditional system of government in vogue at the time emphasised personal allegiance and considered the state oath as the source of a king's judicial authority. Thus an Akuapem man resi-dent in Akyem Abuakwa was liable to stand trial before an Akyem court only if he swore the *okyenhene's* oath or had it sworn upon him. For example, in 1865 Atta Kwaku, brother of Adontehene Ampao, swore the oath of the *okyenhene* and akuapemhene in a dispute with the *Maasehene* over land near Ahabante (near present day Tikong). As two oaths were involved, the case was tried in succession at two separate courts, first before the *akuapemhene's* court at Akropong and then before the *okyenhene's* court at Kyebi. Under such an arrangement it was possible for the Dwaben exiles to live at Kyebi in the 1830s and the Kotoku at nearby Gyadam for 36 years in relative harmony. The Abuakwa owed personal allegiance to the *okyenhene*, invariably swore his oath and took their cases to his court. Similarly, the immigrants swore the oath of their respective kings and took their cases before them.

> With the promulgation of the NJO (1883) the basis of jurisdiction was altered. Henceforth jurisdiction was given a strong territorial definition since the proc-lamation empowered the kings to exercise jurisdiction over territory in their supervision, that is, within the boundaries of their respective states.

The creation of the Native Jurisdiction Ordinance and the imposition of colonial rule created new implications for administration. Akyem Abuakwa was no longer defined in terms of the people accepting allegiance to the Okyenhene. It was now a territorial entity whose borders were drawn up by colonial cartographers and identified as the domain of the Okyenhene. However, far more significant for the administration of land, than mis-guided European conceptions of African traditional rule, was the new eco-nomic wealth which was arising from land. By the late nineteenth and early twentieth century Akyem Abuakwa had become a major centre of export agriculture and concession hunting for gold and diamonds.

The commodification of agrarian production in the early twentieth century

In the late nineteenth century Akyem Abuakwa had a weak agricultural production base. Agriculture was mainly geared towards self-provisioning and gold production was a more important commodity producing sector for the rural population. In his reports on journeys through what now constitutes the Eastern Region Captain Brandon Kirby depicts the Krobo and Akuapem areas as largely farming and oil palm production centres with some cloth production. In contrast with this most of the Akyem Abuakwa and Kotoku towns he passed through are depicted as essentially gold mining towns experiencing decline:

> The population of Eastern Akim [Akyem Abuakwa] is very uncertain, a great influx taking place during the Gold Mining season. There appears, with the exception of Gold Mining and a little Palm Oil Making, no other industry. The towns as a rule show signs of poverty, and there appear to have been no attempts to make roads in any part of the country.[3]

With the proclamation of the end of slavery on the Gold Coast in 1874, the nobility of Akyem Abuakwa were particularly badly hit by desertions from their base of retainers. Mohr, estimated that over 2,000 people claimed their freedom in Abuakwa and left for various parts of the country. At Kyebi "hundreds of slaves … deserted their masters upon hearing of the emancipation proclamation". More than 200 belonged to the Okyenhene. Addo-Fening (1997:30) is keen to depict slavery in Abuakwa as benign, and argues that "only a few slaves in Akyem Abuakwa showed eagerness initially to avail themselves of the Slave Emancipation Act". However, he admits that : "The exodus of freed slaves from the state capital reduced its population drastically and worsened the problem of scarcity of food supply" (1997:66). He also states: "with the loss of their main economic support, most of the inhabitants of Kyebi abandoned the town to live on their farmlands, while the king's wives took up residence at Apedwa. Trading activity and gold-mining almost ground to a halt"(1997:75).

Deprived of labour, many Akyem nobles fell into debt. This particularly affected chiefs who were expected to exhibit largesse and support festivals. Unable to recruit labour for farming or other economic enterprises many chiefs took to selling land to alleviate their debt. Thus evidence provided for an enquiry into the destoolment of Ohene Gyamara of Begoro in 1913 states: "When Jamara came to the stool he borrowed £33 from Konor E. Mate Kole

---

[3] GNA Adm1/645 Journey through Eastern Akim, Enclosure 2 in Despatch no. 14, 24th January 1992, "Itinerary of Brendon Kirby, 24th January 1882 in Despatches from Governor to Secretary of State, January 1882 to March 1882.

[the paramount chief of Manya Krobo] to keep the yam custom and agreed to sell him the Dabetan land to settle the debt".[4]

As international palm oil prices collapsed in the second half of the nineteenth century, following the opening of oil palm plantations in southeast Asia and the discovery of petroleum oil which replaced vegetable oils as a flux in industrial production, prosperous oil palm merchant farmers sought to diversify production. Cocoa was the most lucrative alternative developed in the Akuapem district. Cocoa thrives in moist forests and little of this type of forest existed within Akuapem. Akuapem farmers moved beyond the Densu river into Akyem Abuakwa and found willing land vendors in the town chiefs in this area (Hill, 1963).

The Akuapem cocoa farmers were joined by Anum, Dangme (from Krobo, Shai, Ningo, Prampram), and Ewe migrants. Dwaben and Kwahu farmers within the Abuakwa area also took up cocoa farming. The early movement of migrant cocoa farmers (Hill, 1963) was followed by migrations of less well endowed farmers and labourers seeking employment within the district, hoping to acquire some savings and purchase a small plot of land on which to grow cocoa.

With the establishment of cocoa plantations and a large demand for labour on these plantations there was a further influx of northern migrants into the Akyem area. This was the result of colonial forced labour and taxation policies, that transformed the north into labour reserves for the south (Konings, 1986; Thomas, 1973; Songsore, 1983; Amanor, 1998). Similar policies in Upper Volta (Burkina Faso) and Togo instigated by the French colonialists to release labour for French colonial public works resulted in a large migration of migrants from these areas into Akyem Abuakwa and other cocoa producing districts (Skinner, 1965; Rouch, 1954).

With this influx of labour into Abuakwa, the Akyem chiefs found a new avenue through which they could gain revenues from cocoa land without alienating it. The chiefs began to give out land on a share contract to migrants. This was known as *abusa* (shared into three). Tenants were given areas of virgin forest to clear on which they made cocoa farms, incurring the costs of clearing the land, purchasing the seed and tending them. The cocoa or the plantation was divided into third shares. The planter took two-thirds of the cocoa and the landowner a third share. In another variant, the plantation was shared into two, and when it came into bearing each party was responsible for harvesting their share. The landowner took two thirds of the plantation and the tenant a third share (Hill, 1956).

---

[4] GNA 11/457 1913 Enquiry into charges against Chief Jamara, Ohene of Begoro, case no. 21 of 1913.

A third variant of the *abusa* system existed in Abuakwa, where the tenant was hired as a caretaker on an already established plantation. The caretakers were essentially hired as labourers. They were responsible for weeding, maintaining and harvesting the cocoa and performing errands for the landowner and received one-third of the harvested cocoa in return. This third variant of *abusa* was the norm on the plantations of citizens working on family lands which they had no right to alienate to non-citizens. Other systems of hiring labour that came into existence in Akyem Abuakwa were the *nokotokoana* system and the annual labourer system. *Nkotokoano* (bag full) system was a piece rate system in which the farm worker received a shilling for every bag of cocoa harvested from the plantation (Hill, 1956). The annual labourer was hired for an annual season. The farm owner provided him with housing, clothing and food and often gave him land on which to establish a food farm. He did other jobs for the farm owner in addition to working on the farm, such as collecting water from streams and wells and pounding *fufu* (the staple food made from plantain and cassava pounded in a mortar). At the end of the harvest period the annual labourer would return to his home town and the farm owner would provide him with his annual wages, with which he could buy commodities to send home.

By the 1920s a substantial area of Akyem Abuakua had been alienated to migrants. In *An Epistle to the Educated Youngman in Akim Abuakwa*, Danquah (1928) comments:

> ... about 98% of the land from the Densu at Nsawam to Densuso (Apedwa) has all been sold away absolutely for all time. ... Lands to the left and right of the Nsawam-Densuso road to a distance of 10–25 miles on either side have been sold. The same tale can be told in the Eastern part of the State [Akyem Abuakwa] on the Krobo boundary; the same tale is now going on in the Northern boundary of the State round about Asuom and you are of course aware that the town of Oda (capital of Western Akim) and surrounding villages are situated on land sold by Akim Abuakwa.

While, this is to be regarded as partly rhetoric, as an argument of the political centre, of which Danquah was part, to justify its attempt to strengthen its control over land matters at the expense of divisional chiefs, large areas of Akyem had been alienated to migrants. In an economic survey of Akyem Abuakwa Hill (1957) found that the majority of cocoa was being tended by *abusa* labourers and that the vast majority of these labourers were of migrant origin. At Kwaben and Banso 94 percent of cocoa was being tended by *abusa* labourers, 93 percent at Anyinam, 87 percent at Abomoso, and 53 percent at Moseaso. The majority of these were migrants from the "Northern Territories" (Northern Ghana and Mossi), Basare (Northern Trans-Volta and Togo), Ewe and Krobo. Only 16 percent of the *abusa* labour comprised local Akyem. By the early 1960s Hunter (1963) estimated that 98.6 percent of the land in the New Suhum (trans-Densu area) was being cultivated by migrants.

By the early twentieth century Akyem Abuakwa was one of the leading centres of cocoa production in the world. The bulk of the cocoa producers and workers were not pure blooded indigenous Akyems (if such a concept exists) but emanated from a large catchment area within the Gold Coast and West Africa, extending from Niger and Mali to the southern areas of Togo. In the nineteenth century the main agrarian production unit in Akyem consisted of household labour and slaves. Under the early period of colonial rule agricultural production by the wealthy in Akyem Abuakwa underwent a crisis with the proclamation against domestic slavery. The chiefs responded by selling land to migrant farmers to defray their debts. The development of a prosperous cocoa economy by migrant large-scale farmers led to the migration of farm labourers into Akyem. Wealthy Akyem farmers and chiefs were able to hire this labour or to engage them in various share contracts to develop their own land into cocoa plantations. In the process various forms of hired labour came to structure agrarian production in Akyem, chiefs were able to emerge as wealthy cocoa farmers, and a large area of land in Akyem Abuakwa was appropriated from common lands that could be accessed by peasant farmers through lineage ties.

The administration of land

During the mid-1880s the Gold Coast became the scene of a gold rush. Following the colonial occupation of Asante, speculators rushed to the Gold Coast to gain gold concessions. Diamonds were discovered at Akwatia in Akyem Abuakaw. The rich mineral lands of Akyem Abuakwa became a centre for concession hunting.

The demand for cocoa farming land and mineral concessions radically altered the relationship of people to land, that is the relationship between the Okyenhene—the heir to the eighteenth century migrant conquerors of the land from the Akwamu; the town chiefs—the heirs to those who opened up the land and established control over the process of settlement, some of them dating back to the Akwamu period and before, and the local Akyem whose lands were invested in the various matrilineages. As Field (1948:7) comments of Akyem Kotoku:

> The new income from mines and land sales means that the land, originally valueless to the *oman* and quite independent of it, has become *linked* to the *oman*. The *oman* does not control or own it, but has acquired a very acute interest (in the non-legal sense) in it.

In the case of Akyem Abuakwa on the eve of colonial rule the Okyenhene had little land under his direct control: most of the land came under the town chiefs (Simensen, 1975; Rathbone, 1993). Thus the Okyenhene had to establish new forms of administration over land to acquire economic interests in the land. The context in which this could be carried out was local administration under colonial rule, and the policy of indirect rule through which British colonialism sought to prop up paramount chiefs who were prepared to become allies in the colonial venture.

British colonialism was also concerned about its lack of control over the natural resources of the colony and the transactions in concessions, which had preceded formal imposition of colonial rule. Attempts to place "waste" land within the colony under the Crown met with hostile opposition from the Gold Coast nascent capitalist class. This class largely consisted of traders and businessmen with interests in concessions and lawyers who had themselves invested in concessions (Dumett, 1998; Rathbone, 1993). This class organised the Gold Coast Aborigines' Protection Society which effectively lobbied against attempts to create a Lands Bill that invested land in the Crown (Amanor, 1998). However, as the principles of Indirect Rule were elucidated as the basis for colonial administration, a form of colonial administration evolved in Ghana in which rural administration was carried out through paramount chiefs. The paramount chiefs became responsible for working out an administration based on their interpretation of custom and tradition, and were able to enact bye-laws rooted in customary law. The chiefs were responsible for hearing legal cases, for mobilising communal labour for public works, and for raising revenues through various forms of taxation. Land was recognised as being vested in paramount chiefs. They were central to land administration, responsible for regulating land transactions, releasing concessions for British mining and timber interests, and in appropriating lands for the creation of forest reserves The ideological basis of the system of Indirect Rule was to be rooted in preserving the culture of peoples against disruptive modernising agents, and the chiefs were the representatives of traditional culture. Custom was to be important in colonial rule, but custom was not a process of fluid adaptation to changing conditions: "customary law must be sanctified by age, and cannot be an innovation".[5] However, major innovations were occurring in the economic base of society.

One of the most important allies for the Gold Coast Administration was the Okyenhene, Nana Ofori Atta of Akyem Abuakwa, who had actively challenged the rights of the ARPS to voice national concerns, and argued that the paramount chiefs were the rightful representations of the people. Ofori Atta sought to create a modern Akyem Abuakwa state, with a strong revenue base derived from control over land. The ideological basis for this

---

[5] GNA ADM 11/1106 Pledging of Farms—Native Customary Law relating to Akyem Abuakwa, Secretary of Native Affairs to Commissioner of Eastern Province, 25 April 1929.

was to be rooted in the conquest of the Akwamu by the Ofori Panyin dynasty. Through this conquest the Okyenhene became heir to the land of Akwamu and distributed the land to his followers. While Akyem settlers had use rights in the land, ultimate ownership was vested in the paramount stool who had rights to revenues from the land and services from their subjects (such as communal labour). These rights included the right to an *abusa* (third) share of the extraordinary wealth of the land, such as minerals, timber, and land sales. Nana Ofori Atta claimed rights to a third of land sales and concessions and rights to levy tax on migrants into Akyem Abuakwa. Cocoa farming migrants in Akyem Abuakwa were liable to pay £1 on every bearing cocoa farm and 10/- on each foodstuff farm. This tax was primarily aimed at Dwaben migrants who had in many instances settled freely in Abuakwa during the nineteenth century.[6] Many people protesting this tax were arrested and tried by the Native Tribunal in Kyebi (Simensen, 1974; Addo-Fening, 1997; Rathbone, 1993). While claiming traditional rights, the revenues which were the subject of these traditional rights were new, the creation of new processes of commodification of land resulting from integration into the emerging international system of capitalist production.

Many town chiefs also contested the rights of the Okyenhene to a percentage of their land sales or interference in land transactions. The most famous case was the Asamankese and Akwatia dispute which revolved around the rights to diamond concessions discovered in 1920. Prior to this, relations between the chief of Asamankese and the Okyenhene were tense as a result of disputes over the rights of the Okyenhene in Asamankese land (Addo-Fening, 1974; 1997). Relations were further complicated by the refusal of the Asamankesehene to comply with the collection of the farm tax imposed on Dwaben and other strangers. Asamankese had large stranger quarters of both Dwaben and Anum who had close relations with the Asamankese people. The chief of Asamankese was also married to a Dwaben woman. For failure to comply with the collection of the tax, the Okyenhene imposed a large fine on the representatives of the chief of Asamankese, which further exacerbated bad relations (Addo-Fening, 1997). With the news of diamonds, the chief of Asamankese acted in concert with the chief of Akwatia and they decided to withdraw their allegiance from Akyem Abuakwa. While the colonial authority refused to recognise the cessation of Asamankese and Akwatia from Akyem it took until 1939 to bring these two towns back into the Abuakwa fold after costly litigation, which revealed the complex heterogeneous identities within Abuakwa. If Ofori Atta claimed rights to these towns through the conquest of Ofori

---

[6] This tax is popularly referred to as the Dwabento, "Dwaben tax".

Panin, in 1919, the Omanhene of New Akwamu also claimed his historical
rights to this land:

> I am sending my messenger to the Chief of Asamangkese, and I have asked
> the said messenger to inspect all lands in possession of my forefathers. And I
> have again asked them to inform all descendants from Akwamu who were
> left behind at Akim Peak to stop selling the land, as I am intending to return
> to my ancient abode (quoted in Wilks, 1958).

There were widespread grievances in Akyem Abuakwa at the attempts by
the Okyenhene to extend his control and revenue base at their expense. The
town chiefs were concerned that political affairs were being centralised at
their expense. Their rights to revenues were being usurped by the Okyenhene, and revenues which in the past would have been redistributed from
the Okyenhene to the town chiefs were being retained by the State Council
(Simensen, 1974; Rathbone, 1993).

Among commoners there were grievances that land was being sold to
the detriment of citizens, that chiefs there placing land that they had no
rights to under cocoa farms, that public funds were being used for their own
personal gain and that communal labour was being over-exploited (Simensen, 1974). Among migrants, there were grievances against extortion of new
revenues from them by the Okyenhene.

By the 1920s the Asafos, the military companies in which all commoners
had in the past been organised, were transformed into politicised bodies
which sought to check abuses of power by chiefs and destooled many chiefs.
In 1932 there was an attempt to destool the Okyenhene (Simensen, 1974;
Rathbone, 1993; Addo-Fening, 1997) The Asafos were increasingly heterogeneous organisations, which were now incorporating representatives from
various migrant groups within Akyem Abuakwa, all united by shared
political and economic grievances (Addo-Fening, 1997).

Akyem Abuakwa, the model native authority state was deeply divided.
It was a heterogeneous society, a microcosm of the Gold Coast, torn by
social cleavages, which did not reflect the image of a pure Akyem ethnic
polity with allegiance to an Akyem aristocracy as was portrayed by its
rulers and colonial administration. This problem was highlighted by Macmillan in the 1940s:

> The Akim country, in particular, has not only scattered aliens as individual
> owners but whole village communities of 'alien' occupants. In many market
> towns, of which Suhum is an often quoted type, the aliens are definitely in the
> majority ... and yet the only local tribunals are those of the home tribe, with
> appeal to the local tribal Paramount. The worst feature of all this is that any-
> thing up to 20 per cent of the population of such towns are Northern Territo-
> ries labourers. ... But the labourers must look for redress of grievances in the
> first instances to a tribal court, which is certainly not their own, and may very
> often be composed if not of their actual employers then of their employers'

friends and relatives... In some of the cocoa country, and certainly in the towns, one-tribe courts are therefore an anachronism. It is a fair inference that successful government in the Gold Coast demands a revision by the Colonial Office of its exclusive devotion to a doctrine of Indirect Rule based on tribal institution. The confusion, finally, as it concerns both land-ownership and those questions of tribal jurisdiction, is constantly spreading to any area newly brought under cocoa, especially in the Western Province, but also in Ashanti and Togoland (Macmillan, 1946:90–91).

By the late 1940s it was generally recognised that indirect rule was inappropriate, and that local government needed to be overhauled. The Coussey Committee (1949) recommended a clear separation of traditional state councils from local authorities. It suggested that one third of the representation on local authorities was appointed directly by the traditional authorities and the other two thirds elected. This was implemented in the 1953 Local Government Ordinance, and further reduced to one sixth in the 1953 Municipal Council Ordinance. With the victory of the Convention People's Party (CPP) in the 1956 election, chiefs were excluded from assuming representation on local councils in 1959, which were now wholly elected.

In Akyem Abuakwa, the Okyenhene rallied behind the United Gold Coast Convention Party (UGCC) and its heir the National Liberation Movement (NLM), but in the 1948 election, it was dealt a major blow when the population of Akyem Abuakwa voted in favour of the Nkrumah led CPP. The diversity of Abuakwa society had exerted its identity and rejected the aristocratic notion of a pure Akan ethnic society projected by the Akyem Abuakwa nobility (Rathbone, 1996). Since the Asantehene and the Okyenhene had both stood resolutely against the CPP, the CPP sought to thwart the powers of these paramount chiefs. In 1958 legislation was introduced to weaken the power base of the *Okyenhene* and in 1959 of the *Asantehene*. The administration of stool revenues in both areas was placed in the hands of a Receiver of Stool Lands revenue. Up to one third of the revenues collected could be used by the Minister of Local Government. In 1960 this was extended to all traditional authorities in the Stool Lands Act. This allowed the President to vest any stool land in the Office of the President when it appeared to be in the "public interest". The 1962 Administration of Lands Act vested all lands in the president and the administration of stool revenues came under the authority of central government which was empowered to determine the proportion of revenues going to the chiefs.

While the struggle of the CPP against the chiefs was fuelled by popular anti-chief sentiments and the wave of destoolments of chiefs during the 1950s, the CPP did little to strengthen popular rights in land administration or introduce popular land reform. It recognised the land as vested in the chiefs and placed it under the control of government to administer on behalf of the chiefs. This was to lead the way for an eventual rapprochement between government and chiefs in which chiefs could be used to alienate land

and to legitimate government appropriation of land for projects (Amanor, 1999).

Chiefs still play an important role in land matters. They gain access to royalties from timber and mining concessions. However, their role in local administration has declined. Local administration is now based on district assemblies. While the Chief Executives of these district assemblies are appointed by central government as are one third of their membership, the Unit Committees representing villages are elected by universal ballot. A number of elected Unit Committees form an Area Committee, which in theory should have a permanent secretariat. The Area Committees are responsible for devising development plans for the area and submitting project proposals to the District Assembly for funding. The Unit Committees have only recently come into being as functioning elected units.

There are tensions in this system between a District Assembly bureaucracy which is appointed by central government and situated in the district capital and elected village committees. Frequently, funding is insufficient to meet the needs of the district and the District Assembly allocates the majority of the funding for the whole district for infrastructure and social infrastructure support in the district capital. However, Unit Committees are increasingly demanding their share of district funding.

For all the shortcomings in the system, a more democratic means of local administration is coming into being. The choice for more appropriate rural development administration is not between some dualist notion of central government or the state and some notion of traditional community organisation. The present struggle for rural development administration is between a democratically elected forum based on a process of popular consultation and participation in development planning within villages and a system of bureaucratic management at the district capital based on appointed officials. Improved popular participation in development can be achieved by strengthening the ability of citizens to articulate their concerns in the Unit Committees, by developing procedures for a more responsive local planning process with checks and balances, and creating a planning process at the district centre based on clear procedures, which will facilitate a process of dialogue between the Unit Committees and the District Assembly, in which the Unit Committees may challenge the decisions of the planning centre.

Commodification of labour and youth in the postcolonial setting

As a result of the movement of migrants in the nineteenth and early twentieth century land and labour markets developed in Akyem. Large areas of land were alienated to migrant farmers, large areas were developed by chiefs using share contracts, and nobles and large farmers could expand their areas of cocoa plantation using migrant labour. By the1960s youth within the Akyem area were faced with serious problems of land shortage. This occurred in a period of serious economic recession in Ghana.

This economic recession was partly a result of declining primary commodity prices on the world market. In the early postwar periods rising prices for cocoa had resulted in an expansion of production. By the mid-1960s prices for cocoa began to fall as new production areas within the world economy began to compete with Ghana, resulting in overproduction. Old areas of cocoa production, such as Akyem, suffered from these falling producer prices, since the cost of maintaining old plantations, rehabilitating old cocoa plantations and replanting them with new hybrid varieties, and managing disease problems[7] resulted in very low profit margins. Many farmers in the Eastern Region began to abandon their cocoa and move into other crops. Within Ghana the main areas of cocoa production shifted into the new frontier areas of Ahafo and the Western Region, where uncultivated primary forest was still to be found.

Declining revenues from cocoa also led to a national economic recession and growing unemployment. The response of the Busia government was to blame this crisis on migrants from other West African nations. In an interview with Cameron Duodu in the *Daily Graphic* of January 19, 1970, Busia said:

> Added to this, of course is the fact that of the people who have registered for work, one out of every four is unemployed. Rising prices and pressures: what were we to do? Then as you know, our estimated population now is about eight million. The aliens also number one million and a half. We know that many of them are in the country without resident permits, because of the policies of the Nkrumah government which seemed to invite everybody at all who liked to come and stay in Ghana. Some of them were even being kept here, housed and fed by the Government, to further his 'imperialist policies.
>
> In a situation like this—there is one other thing too that I must add to that which I musn't forget—our prison records show that 90% of those who were on the books for the last year for which we have complete statistic—1968—90% of those in prison, especially for criminal things like robbery with violence and so on, were aliens. ...
>
> Also a number of people had noticed aliens who were unemployed and engaged in stealing. And some were engaged in the petty trading in foodstuffs and the rest. So people began to ask why there were so many aliens here. This is a question that no popularly elected government can ignore. So we said let our laws be fulfilled. We have regulations and those aliens who have come without residence papers must obtain them.

---

[7] During the 1940s the swollen-shoot epidemic developed in Eastern Region cocoa. This could only be dealt with by cutting out diseased cocoa and replanting it with swollen-shoot resistant hybrid varieties.

At the end of 1969 aliens were given two weeks in which to register, and after hundreds of thousands were expelled. While the expulsion of West African migrants, focussed on petty traders whose assets were taken over by Ghanaians and the informal sector, the expulsion rapidly moved into the agricultural sector and thousands of labourers on cocoa plantations were forced to leave. This raised concerns about supplies of cheap farm labour. A *Daily Graphic* report of 28 January 1970, "Police Probe Aliens Bribe Report" stated:

> Mr Kofi Genfi III, MP for Atwima Amansie, yesterday called on the govern-
> ment to make it abundantly clear that alien farm labourers were privileged to
> stay in Ghana. Mr Gyemfi said it appeared the Government Compliance
> Order was being misapplied by some unscrupulous people in the rural areas.
> Addressing a news conference in Kumasi, Mr Gyemfi said he had received
> complaints from some farmers that there were people going around the
> villages asking farm labourers to leave the country. As a result many labour-
> ers have left for their countries and this has put some farmers in a difficult
> position. "If the Government does nothing to arrest the alarming situation
> which is rearing its head, the cocoa industry will seriously be at stake" he
> said.

Since the Aliens Compliance Order labour shortfalls have become a serious problem in the forest belt (Adomako-Safo, 1974; Addo, 1972). Ghanaian migrants and local youth have moved in to replace Sahelian migrant labour, but these tend to work as casual labourers rather than annual or permanent labourers (Adomako-Safo, 1974). Many local youth also work under share-cropping contracts. After the removal of the Busia government, there were moves to attempt to encourage migrant Sahelian labour back into the cocoa economy. However, these moves were rejected by rural youth. Adomako-Safo (1974:152) reports that "many [youth] have already demonstrated against the return of the aliens after the change of government following the announcement by the new military leaders [the Acheampong led National Redemption Council] that the Aliens Compliance Order would be re-viewed".

The forceful expulsion of non-Ghanaian West African farm labourers, did not significantly transform the heterogeneous nature of Akyem society. Communities of migrants who had previously settled in Akyem Abuakwa continued to exist. However, it altered the nature of farm labour. Farm labour was no longer the preserve of annual labourers who performed serv-ices for their landowners and received wages after the harvest with which to go home. This form of cheap labour was now replaced by a more expensive system of daily hired labour and contract labour. Farmers who could not afford to pay for labour were forced to release their land to youth on share-crop arrangements. Local youth had participated in the expulsion of "alien" labour to gain a niche for themselves as labourers and sharecroppers, to push out cheap labour with which they could not compete.

This led to a structural transformation in agricultural production. With few employment activities outside of agriculture and increasing shortage of land, youth sought freedom from a long service to their elders as farm hands, without much scope for gaining land of their own. By gaining a niche as labourers and sharecroppers, youth could gain a source of income and more freedom than working for their family elders. However, the result of this is that the "family farm" has broken down as a unit, and agriculture is increasingly an economic activity carried out by individuals who hire labour to supplement their own efforts. The relationship between youth and elders is now defined by commodity production, with elders representing land and youth labour.

This commodification of youth labour has led to a moral crusade against youth, who are portrayed as disrespectful to their elders and lazy (shirking manual labour on the farm). In this discourse the roots of youth migration lie in laziness, the search for easy work outside of the agricultural sector. As a result of increasing lack of respect for elders among youth, youth no longer help their ageing fathers on the farm, but work as casual agricultural labour on other people's land.

Conclusion

This overview of agriculture in the Akyem Abuakwa areas shows that the agrarian structure is complex and dynamic, and has consistently changed in relation to changes in the material base of production and incorporation into the world market. These transformations have brought about a series of conflicts between different social categories of producers and increasing commodification in production and exchange relations. The commodification of land resulted in a conflict between paramount chiefs, subchiefs and commoners and brought migrants into Abuakwa as land purchasers. The development of cocoa farming brought migrants from colonial labour reserves into Abuakwa as annual labourers and sharecrop tenants. Increasing land shortage created a crisis for youth, which brought them into the agrarian economy as daily and contract labour displacing long-distance labour migrants.

The development of this economy has preceded through conflicts between different social forces. Since the colonial period, the dominant forces have attempted to justify their position through recourse to the concept of tradition. In creating a framework for the land question based on concepts of community and traditional management, whose traditions are going to be utilised? Is it the traditions of chiefs, sub-chiefs, commoners, migrants, or youth?

The central concern of this work is to examine the implications of imposing concepts of community management drawn from global liberal concerns onto a situation of social transformation in agricultural production, in which different interests are competing to defend and strengthen their positions in the contemporary flux.

Chapter 2
Two Types of Cocoa Settlement

In *Migrant Cocoa Farmers* Polly Hill (1963) draws attention to two distinct types of cocoa economy found in Akyem Abuakwa. The first is the small peasant cocoa farmer, popularised by Beckett (1947) in *Akokoaso: A Survey of a Gold Coast Cocoa Village*, often farming around a couple of acres of cocoa. The second is the large migrant farmers who often combined cocoa with trading. Capital which was consolidated in the oil palm trade was used to purchase land and open up migrant settlements specifically for cocoa farming. This chapter examines the changing fortunes of these two types of areas more than one hundred years after the opening of the cocoa economy. It examines two settlements situated in the Atewa Range which correspond to the small farmer type and one archetype migrant pioneer cocoa settlement in the New Suhum area, which featured in Hill's *Migrant Cocoa Farmers*. After years of recession, slump in cocoa prices and structural adjustment measures how do these two types of settlement fair? This chapter provides an introduction to these villages. It examines changes in the economies of these areas and the centrality of cocoa to their way of life.

Atewa Range settlements

Apinaman and Dwenease are neighbouring settlements situated at the foot of the Atewa Range in the area towards Akwatia, a major diamond winning town in Ghana. Gold deposits have also been abundant in the area. They are situated near the line of old Akwamu heartland towns. The distance between the lines of houses that make up these settlements is a ten minute walk.

The people of Apinaman are Akyems of the Asona *abusuakese* (clan), who trace their origins to Adanse. They originally settled in the Dabinase area, in the northwest of Abuakwa. Here they were experiencing water problems so they sent hunters into the Atewa Range where they found a large stream (*osuobranin*). They then moved to settle at their present site on land bordering that claimed by Akanteng, an old Akwamu town.[8]

---

[8] The meaning of Apinaman is 'yen peri aman'—we are drawing nearer to a town, i.e. Akateng.

Figure 2.1 *The Settlement*

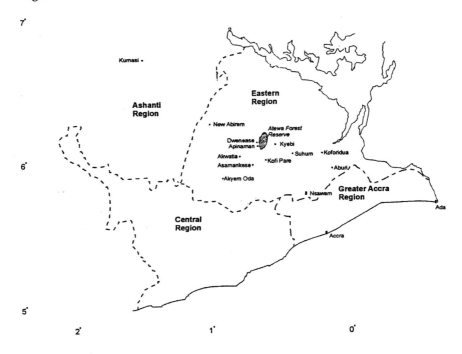

The people of Dwenease are also Akyems, but from the Oyoko clan. They trace their origins to Adanse and moved from there to Nkwantanan during the Asante-Denkyira wars. Some of their historical oral traditions claim that their ancestors came to settle under a Odwen tree in the 1830s led by Twumbarima. But they were constantly harassed by wild animals and so they retreated to Nkwantanan. Eventually some of them returned to rebuild their settlement around the Odwen tree, hence the name of the settlement Dwenease (under the Odwen tree). But Apinaman people were now claiming the land and this led to open conflict. Dwenease people recount how six Dwenease men were able to withstand the might of Apinaman and maintain their settlement. While the concern of this narrative may be to establish a priori claims to land,
between Apinaman and

The Dwenease peo
people rushed to delil
stake a claim to owne
century, Dwenease peo
land to migrant farme

Table 2.1 *Service sector activities in the Atewa Range settlements*

Services	No. at Apinaman	No. at Dwenease
Provision shops	27	5
Hairdressers	19	7
Tailors/seamstresses	22	6
Carpenters	16	5
Masons	23	30
Chemist shops	4	2
Beer bars	6	4
Akpeteshie spirit bars	26	11
Chop bars	4	2
Petrol/Diesel sellers	3	1
Chainsaw operators	8	3

people are now experiencing serious land shortage. They feel hemmed in by lands claimed by Apinaman, and the government forest reserve, an official no-go area—which like many forest reserves is being surreptitiously farmed. Land shortage also exists at Apinaman, but it is not as generally prevalent as at Dwenease. It is more focussed on poorer households and youth.

Population and migration

Apinaman is the larger farming settlement. In the 1984 census its population was estimated at 2,607 and 310 houses were counted. Dwenease was entered for 1,376 people and 170 houses in the same sample. The different sizes of these towns is reflected in the provision of tertiary services. Apinaman supports a much wider variety of shop fronts and workshops than Dwenease. Apinaman also has a lively night food market where kenkey, fish, banku, rice, fried eggs and bread, among other foods are sold. This night activity becomes the focus of social life, of the evening stroll, which most youth take up and down the main street. On festive occasions bands come to perform at Apinaman, electrifying the atmosphere with generators. Both towns will soon be on the electricity grid and electric poles are busily being erected now. The youth of Dwenease usually gravitate towards Apinaman in the evenings. By nine in the evening Dwenease is quiet in slumber while the streets and bars of Apinaman are bustling with life.

The population of these two towns is highly mobile. There is a constant movement of people in and out of these settlements. A large number of people born and bred in Apinaman and Dwenease live and work outside. This is most evident at funerals when large numbers of citizens come from outside to swell the populations of the various houses. A large number of people also constantly move between city and these rural towns. Sometimes they will be found in Accra, where they squat with resident family members. They often carry out informal sector activities, such as petty trading, and hawking wares along the streets of Accra. Few of them are able to play significant roles in the marketing of agricultural produce within the Accra markets, since these are heavily controlled by large traders and "market queens", who control powerful political networks within the market that enable them to exert monopoly control over the marketing of commodities within the major market places.

The proximity of Accra—a two hour minibus journey—results in the capital city being a magnet for a large proportion of the Atewa Range population. Many of the sons and daughters of these two settlements are resident in Accra, but they sometimes come back in the farming season to make farms to supplement their income. An example is Yaw Tenkora, a 36 year old man from Dwenease:

> I am doing a little selling in Accra. I only come to make a farm here in the farming season and then return to Accra. I don't have land here. I am only feeding on it. Its not mine. Its my father's land. He has two and a half acres of cocoa on it for himself. I clear about one acre of my father's land and plant plantain, cocoyam, cassava and some maize.

In a survey of children born to women residents in Apinaman and Dwenease, it was found that the majority of children over the age of 17 were living outside of these settlements. Of 115 children over the age of 17 born to 25 women at Apinaman, 43 percent were resident within a 15 km radius of the settlement. Of the 57 percent living outside the locality 24 percent were based in Accra, 19 percent in the Eastern Region (of which 13 percent were in other Akyem towns), 4 percent in the Ashanti Region, 3 percent in the Northern and Upper Regions, 1 percent in the Western Region, and 2 percent in other West African countries. Of 101 children over 17 years of age born to 20 women at Dwenease 35 percent resided in a 15 km radius of their home town, 25 percent within Accra, 25 percent in Eastern Region towns (of which 23 percent were situated in Akyem territory) 12 percent within the Ashanti Region, 2 percent within the Western Region and 1 person had migrated to Brong Ahafo and another to Europe. Accra was the most important magnet for migration, but a sizeable portion moved to other Eastern Region towns, most of which were situated in the Akyem area.

In both settlements the most common work carried out by these children to resident mothers was farming, "government work" (popularly used to define salaried or wage labour mainly for government agencies but it now includes private sector firms and privatised former public sector firms), and trading. This was followed by a cluster of artisans, including carpenters, masons, roadside mechanics, garment makers and hairdressers. At Apinaman more of these children were involved in agriculture, and at Dwenease a larger proportion worked for government services.

Table 2.2 *Occupations of migratory descendants of Atewa Range resident mothers*

Occupation	Apinaman (%)	Dwenease (%)
Farming	30	23
"Government work"	15	23
Trading	11	17
Mason	4	3
Carpenter	4	1
Seamstress	3	1
Roadside mechanic	3	
Hairdresser	4	5
Housewife	3	11
Student	4	2

Table 2.3 *Primary occupations at Apinaman and Dwenease*

Primary occupation	Apinaman			Dwenease		
	Male	Female	Total	Male	Female	Total
Farmer	96	63	80	86	53	73
Helping parents on farm	.	8	4	.	11	4
Petty trader	.	17	8	3	26	8
Garment maker	.	8	4	.	.	.
Hairdresser	.	4	2	.	11	4
Chainsaw operator	4	.	2	3	.	2
Other	.	.	.	8	4	7
No. of respondents	26	24	50	29	19	48

Table 2.4 *Secondary occupations at Apinaman and Dwenease*

Secondary occupation	Apinaman			Dwenease		
	Male	Female	Total	Male	Female	Total
None	50	50	50	52	26	42
Farmer	.	21	10	10	32	19
Petty trading	23	29	26	10	37	21
Artisan	8	.	4	7	.	4
Chainsaw operator	3	.	2	.	.	.
Gold mining	12	.	6	.	.	.
Diamond mining	.	.	.	3	.	2
Other	4	.	3	12	5	12
No. of respondents	26	24	50	29	19	48

Employment and livelihood

The dominant occupation in these settlements is farming. Between 50–60 percent of the population combine agriculture with some other secondary occupation. The most common secondary occupation is petty trading. A significant number of women consider petty trading to be their primary occupation and agriculture to be a secondary occupation. Petty trading includes prepared food vending, selling of agricultural commodities, alcoholic drinks and minerals, and common industrially produced commodities such as soap, tinned foods, sugar, cigarettes, rope, nails, and confectionery. At Apinaman 63 percent of women respondents considered agriculture to be their primary occupation as compared with 96 percent of the men. At Dwenease 53 percent of women considered agriculture to be their primary occupation as compared to 86 percent of the men. In both settlements a significant number of young women (8–11 percent) considered that they had no occupation of their own and were helping their parents to farm. This gender difference in relation to work within the agricultural sector reflects the greater difficulty women face in gaining access to land and labour for farming. Other significant primary occupations include garment making, hairdressing and chainsaw work. Beyond this are a number of government employees, such as school teachers, agricultural extension staff, etc. Other secondary occupations include artisans, such as carpenters and masons, who cannot find sufficient demand for their skills locally to work full time and gold mining and diamond winning and chainsaw activities.

In addition to secondary occupations, people also engage in more ephemeral activities. These include casual labour on farms, goldmining, and carrying beams for chainsaw operators. At Apinaman 68 percent of men engage in casual farm labour ("by day") hiring themselves out by the day. No women engage in "by day". In the Dwenease survey significantly fewer people engaged in "by day". Only 19 percent of men work as casual farm labour, but 11 percent of women also engage in "by day".

Goldmining is another important supplementary income generating activity, and in the past was a major job for Apinaman people. During the colonial period informal sector mining was made illegal. Nevertheless, it continued. It was not until 1989 that it was legalised under the influence of neo-liberal ideologies and promotion of export growth. However, as concession areas have been rapidly extended to large scale foreign enterprise, small scale miners have again begun to work in the illegal sector as their lands have been given out as concessions. Around Apinaman and Dwenease gold deposits have recently become exhausted and people wishing to work in goldmining have to migrate to other areas. Two types of gold mining occurs: pit mining in deep shafts that are dug out manually and alluvial gold mining, which involves panning streams. Both men and women participate in gold mining. Usually there is a division of labour in which the men dig the striate and women sift and wash the soil for gold deposits. At Apinaman 56 percent of the sample have been involved in gold mining activities, including 54 percent of men and 58 percent of women. At Dwenease 29 percent of the sample had engaged in gold mining including 31 percent of men and 26 percent of women.

A third important source of irregular income comes from carrying the beams of timber sawn up by chainsaw operators from forest and fallow land to the roadside. Much of this activity is illegal, or has been illegalised by recent legislation. At Apinaman 16 percent of the survey carried boards including 19 percent of men and 16 percent of women. At Dwenease 17 percent carried boards including 21 percent of men and 11 percent of women. Carrying boards and gold mining is generally preferred to casual labour, since it provides more money for less work. However, board carrying is a strenuous activity.

These three activities have provided important sources of income for the youth. Carrying boards and gold mining, are also important in providing alternatives for the youth to farming and to farm labour, and dependence on elders for employment as farm labour.

Agriculture and the farming system

In both Apinaman and Dwenease farmers plant plantation and food crops. The main plantation crops are cocoa, oil palm and citrus, with cocoa predominating. The main food crops consist of an intercrop of plantain, cassava and cocoyam to which can be added other crops such as pepper and garden eggs, or yams or maize. Other cropping systems consist of pure stands of maize or an intercrop of maize and cassava. In recent years, some young farmers have been experimenting with growing dry season garden eggs in moist valley bottoms, and also rice which some of the youth have learnt from the rice growing areas in western Akyem.[9]

In the early years of plantation development, the plantation crops are combined with food crops for up to about three years. After that, the plantation crops begin to establish themselves and create shade under which food crops cannot grow well. The farm is then left as a pure stand or orchard. Oil palm plantations last about 25 years, cocoa around 40 years and citrus orchards 50 years and more. Originally cocoa was the main plantation crop, until it began to suffer from problems of senescence and the swollen shoot epidemic. Swollen shoot has necessitated the replanting of cocoa and the replacement of original *amelonado* varieties with *amazonia* and hybrids. Re-

---

[9] The area has high rainfall as a result of the mountainous and forested Atewa Range that lies behind the towns.

planting is expensive, and the producer and world market prices of cocoa have declined relatively since the 1970s. This has resulted in many farmers moving out of cocoa into the other plantation crops or increasingly depending on food crops for their main cash income.

Orchards have more prestige than food farms, since they create a source of wealth which can be passed on as inheritance (*egyapadie*), as an achievement of a particular individual. The process of creating a plantation alienates land to the plantation owner for the life of the plantation. In contrast food crops are more ephemeral. After six years of cultivating plantains, the farm has to be fallowed as it becomes depleted of nutrients. The process of creating wealth on that land can only begin again once the land has rested and restored its fertility, and then the wealth is only fleeting, perpetually being recycled from plot to plot. Thus, no property is created on food plots by farmers.

A large number of farmers have some area of orchard crops. At Apinaman 68 percent of men and 60 percent of women had some area of orchard and 81 percent of men and 70 percent of women at Dwenease. Those without plantations are usually young farmers who have not as yet established themselves as farmers. By the time most farmers reach their forties they have some area of plantation. There is no significant difference in gender participation in plantation development. Figure 2.2 shows the distribution of mature plantation in the Atewa Range settlements and figure 2.3 shows the various crops that people were planting on their newly cleared farms in the 1999/2000 farm season.

While most farmers have plantations, these plantations are small. The vast majority of plantations are under 5 acres. Of the farmers who could estimate the size of their cocoa only 12 percent at Apinaman had more than 5 acres. No women had more than 5 acres. At Dwenease 27 percent of cocoa holdings were above 5 acres, including 34 percent of male holdings and 11 percent of women's cocoa holdings. No woman had more than 20 acres of land at Dwenease. 65 percent of all cocoa holdings at Apinaman and 40 percent at Dwenease were 2 acres and below. The greater land shortage at Dwenease results in fewer women having plantations than men and most women who have plantations have very small areas—78 percent have areas of 2 acres and less. The majority of cocoa grown in these Atewa Range settlements provides a supplementary income rather than the major farm income.

Land at Kofi Pare

Kofi Pare is a settlement of migrants situated in the New Suhum area to the south of the Atewa Range. Its core comprises farmers who point their origins to Aburi in Akuapem. This group identifies itself as the descendants of Kofi Pare, the original purchaser of the land, who became the *asafohene* (captain/commoner chief) of the land. Kofi Pare approached the chief of Akanteng (a neighbouring town of Apinaman) for the land situated at Wansambirampa (the name of the stream) in 1911. The area purchased was 1,525 acres. The cost of the land was £400 plus boundary cutting costs of £100 (Hill, 1963).

Figure 2.2 *Distribution of mature plantations in the Atewa Range*

Farmers with plantation at Apinaman

Men

	Under 25	26-35	36-45	46-60	Over 60	Total
No plantation						8
Cocoa						16
Oil palm.						6
Citrus						2
Percentage of farmers with plantation		50%	67%	73%	100%	68%
No of farmers	4	9	11	1		25

Women

	Under 25	26-35	36-45	46-60	Over 60	Total
No plantation						8
Cocoa						11
Oil palm						2
Percentage of farmers with plantation		25%	100%	100%	75%	60%
No of farmers	1	8	2	5	4	20

Farmers with plantation at Dwenease

Men

	Under 25	26-35	36-45	46-60	Over 60	Total
No plantation						5
Cocoa						18
Oil palm.						10
Citrus						6
Percentage of farmers with plantation	50%	73%	75%	100%	100%	81%
No of farmers	2	11	4	3	6	26

Women

	Under 25	26-35	36-45	46-60	Over 60	Total
No plantation						13
Cocoa						25
Oil palm						10
Citrus						6
Percentage of farmers with plantation	67%	67%	70%	25%	86%	70%
No of farmers	3	12	10	4	14	43

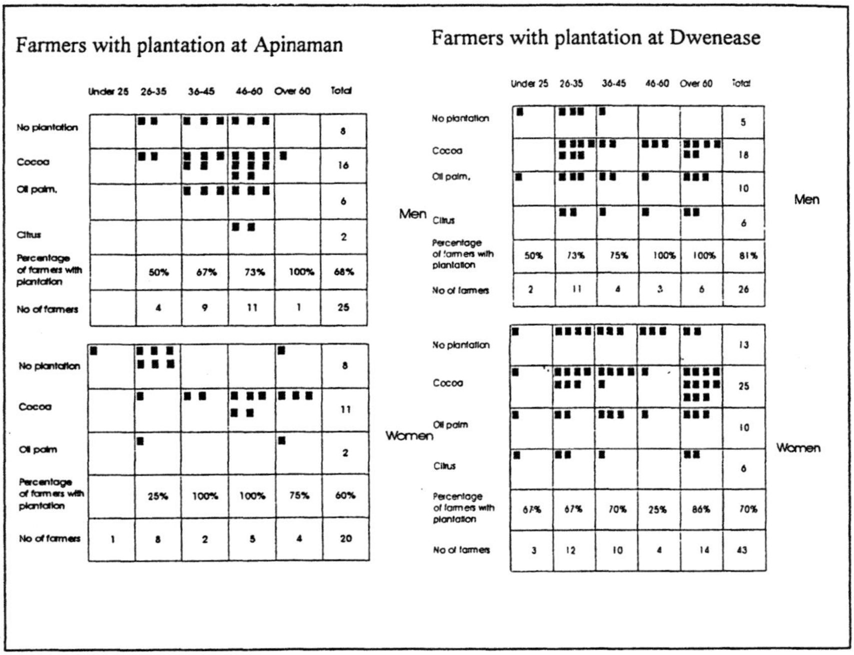

Table 2.5 *Estimated size of plantations in the Atewa Range settlements*

Area under plantation
crops

2 acres and less
2–5 acres
5–20 acres
Over 20 acres
No. of farmers

Figure 2.3 *Crops planted in the 1999/2000 season*

Apinaman

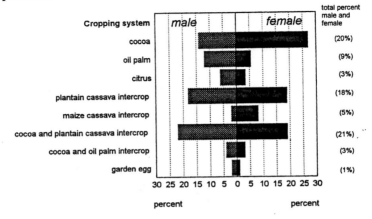

Dwenease

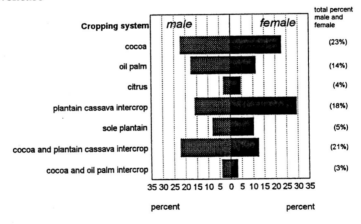

Kofi Pare features in Polly Hill's *Migrant Cocoa Farmers of Southern Ghana*, in Appendix III. 4: The Kofi Pare Family Land. However, the shape of Kofi Pare has changed from the days of Hill's survey, for since then other migrants—including Akuapem people from Larteh, Dangme people mainly from Shai and Krobo and Ewes—who occupied lands adjacent to Kofi Pare, have moved into the outskirts of the town and built their houses there. These farmers are intimately connected with the Aburi section, sharecropping and labouring on their lands, and providing services including food selling, palm tapping, *akpeteshie* distilling, etc. There are also a few "northerners", people from the savannah regions of northern Ghana, Niger and Mali, who originally came to Kofi Pare as annual labourers. The Akuapem population from Aburi, perhaps makes up 70 percent of the population, people from Larteh in Akuapem make up another 10 percent, Dangmes and Ewes accounting for about 15 percent, and the "northerners" another five percent.

The descendants of Kofi Pare trace their origins back to Sakyikrom and Nsakyi and to Akwamu, from where it is claimed that Kofi Pare's maternal grandfather originated. From there, Kofi Pare's father, Nana Danso, his junior brother, Mensah Akoanankrom and Kofi Pare purchased land at Pakro (Parekrom). The profits which Kofi Pare gained from farming at Pakro were used to purchase land at Kofi Pare.

Hill records that Kofi Pare had six associates with whom he purchased the land. These associates were all related, although they were not all matrilineal relatives. Four of the groups came from Kofi Pare's maternal side and three from other matrilineages. The land was divided among these seven associates according to their contribution. These seven associates subsequently divided their share among their relatives, giving portions to both matrilineal and patrilineal relatives. These seven sections remain distinct to this day. The lands within these sections have not been parcelled out into subdivided plots apportioned to the next generation. The descendants have gained rights to the use of land, rather than to particular plots of land. Cocoa farms are inherited rather than the land. Thus the subdivision of land into plots claimed by particular people follows the extension and contraction of plantations. Hill (1963) records that in 1959 there were 137 farmers registered as owning land within the surveyed area and 49 farmers within Kofi Pare's section. Today there are about 45 farmers with claims to ownership of farms within the Kofi Pare section, of which five are women. The land has been inherited by both children and maternal relatives of Kofi Pare.

When Kofi Pare first came to the land, he was followed by his brother Kwadjo Danso and his maternal nephews Yaw Kwafo and Yaw Akotuah. The nephews helped Kofi Pare on his farms and Kofi Pare gave them land on which to make their own cocoa farms. They would take time off from working on Kofi Pare's land to establish their own farms. These farms were inherited by their nephews and children who in turn had helped them to establish their own farms. Both children (in the paternal line) and matrilineal relatives have inherited land at Kofi Pare.

Kofi Pare did not only rely on his relatives to establish his cocoa farms. He also had many labourers working for him, including Fantis, Wangaras, Chambas, Zambarama, and some Akuapem. Some of these were rewarded for service with plots of land. For instance, Kwame Owu came to work as a labourer for Kofi Pare. He worked hard, but could not save enough money to purchase his own land, so Kofi Pare eventually rewarded him with a plot of land. Many other landowners at Kofi Pare have also relied on caretakers to manage their farm and have been absentee farmers. Thus, in the heyday of cocoa migrant labourers made up a significant part of Kofi Pare's population. Through his labourers, Kofi Pare was able to extend his own cocoa plantations and maintain existing farms.

During the 1940s the cocoa in Kofi Pare was attacked by swollen shoot disease. As a result of this several farmers abandoned their farms. In 1959, when Hill carried out her survey, only 59 of the registered farm-owners were resident at Kofi Pare. A further 39 farmers were resident in the Akuapem area on other farms, from where they paid regular visits to their lands at Kofi Pare. Of the remaining 43 farmers, only 18 were reported to be living in cocoa growing areas, mainly in Akyem, and the location of the others was unknown, since they were not visiting their farms regularly.

Population and migration

In 1948 the population of Kofi Pare with associated villages was 1,626. In the 1984 census this was 1,403. The population has declined. This may partly be the result of the decline of cocoa following the swollen shoot epidemic and the movement of migrant cocoa labourers and caretakers to other frontier cocoa areas in the Western Region of Ghana. Labourers from neighbouring Sahelian countries also moved to the Côte d'Ivoire, where they helped open up the cocoa industry that came to eclipse Ghanaian production because of more favourable conditions for migrants in the 1970s and 1980s than in post-Aliens Compliance Order Ghana.[10] Lack of available land and an inheritance system that does not fragment holdings would also encourage migration of youth and the land hungry to other cocoa farming or out of agriculture.

In a survey of children born to 26 women resident at Kofi Pare it was found that the majority of them were residing outside of Kofi Pare. Only 24

[10] At the time when migrants were being expelled from Ghana, Côte d'Ivoire was welcoming Burkina and Malian migrants and allowing them to own land under the principle of land to the cultivator.

percent of the 75 children above the age of 17 remained at Kofi Pare or within a 15 km radius. 24 percent had moved to other settlements in the Eastern Region, 29 percent to the Greater Accra Region, 8 percent to the Western Region, 7 percent to the Ashanti Region, 4 percent to the Volta region 1 percent to Brong Ahafo and 3 percent to other countries in West Africa. The most important town which absorbed migration was Accra which had become the residence of 27 percent of the children. Koforidua, the Eastern Region capital, accounted for 5 percent, and Kumase was the magnet for 4 percent. The home towns in Akuapem were also important for some people and 5 percent of the children were settled there.

The most important economic activities carried out by these children are farming (20 %) hairdressing (7 %) dressmaking (6 %) masonry (5 %), trading (8 %), keeping a store (4%) and food selling and drink retailing. Five percent of the sample were also employed in government departments such as agricultural and cocoa services. Women who had gone to stay with their husbands and establish families were also a significant category (12 %). Most of the artisans were migrants while the majority of those farming remained in Kofi Pare.

The tertiary services available at Kofi Pare include stores, chop bars, tailors, hairdressers, blacksmiths, chainsaw operators, drinking and *akpeteshie* bars and chemist shops and cocoa buying warehouses. Government services include primary and Junior Secondary Schools (JSS) schools and a clinic.

Table 2.6 *Service sector activities at Kofi Pare*

Services	Number at Kofi Pare
Provision shops	5
Hairdressers	9
Tailors/seamstresses	3
Carpentry workshops	6
Masons	5
Blacksmiths	3
Chainsaw operators	6
Chop bars	3
Drinking bars (serving alcohol and minerals)	3
Akpeteshie spirit bars	13
Chemist shops	3

Employment and livelihood

The majority of people at Kofi Pare are farmers. In a survey of 59 farmers 80 percent gave their main occupation as farming. Other important primary occupations included petty trading (in food stuffs, fish, and commodities originating from urban areas and import), owning a store, and selling cooked foods. Men are more reliant on farming than women with 91 percent counting agriculture as their primary livelihood as compared to 65 percent of women. For women petty trading, dressmaking, hairdressing and food processing are important economic activities that provide alternative forms of livelihood to agriculture.

Table 2.7 *Primary occupations of Kofi Pare residents*

Primary occupation	Male (%)	Female (%)	Frequency	Percent
Farmer	91	65	47	80
Petty trader	6	12	5	9
Storekeeper	3		1	2
Cooked food seller		4	1	2
Seamstress/tailor		4	1	2
Hairdresser		8	2	3
Oil palm processor		4	1	2
Herbalist		4	1	2
Total no.	33	26	59	100

49 percent of the sample were totally reliant on agriculture including 64 percent of men and 31 percent of women. Women are more likely to combine agriculture with a secondary occupation than men. 31 percent of women also regard agriculture as a secondary occupation, compared to 9 percent of men. The main secondary occupations for women are petty trading, dressmaking, and food processing. The main secondary occupations for men are distilling, and artisan crafts like carpentry and masonry. There is not sufficient demand to sustain many full time artisans. All the residents were either farming as a primary or secondary occupation with the exception of one woman in the 25–35 year age category who worked full time as a hairdresser. Thus the population of Kofi Pare are highly dependent upon agriculture. The greater reliance of women on complementary off-farm incomes probably reflects their more marginal access to land and capital for farm operations.

Agriculture and the farming system

As in the Atewa Range settlements, the dominant crops grown at Kofi Pare are cocoa and food crops. However, a wider range of food crops are grown in Kofi Pare than in the Atewa Range settlements. Sugar cane is an important cash crop at Kofi Pare, which is often grown in valley bottoms. Sugar cane competes with oil palm cultivation and vegetables in the valley bottoms. The plantain cassava intercrop is less significant here than in the

Atewa Range settlements, and larger quantities of maize and cassava are being grown as sole stands and as an intercrop.

Table 2.8 *Secondary occupations of Kofi Pare residents*

Secondary occupation	Male (%)	Female (%)	Total no.	Percent
None	64	31	29	49
Farmer	9	31	11	19
Petty trader	9	23	9	15
Carpenter/mason	6		2	3
Tailor/seamstress		8	2	3
Distiller	9		3	5
Food seller		1	1	2
Palm oil processor		4	1	2
Pastor	3		1	2
Total no.	33	26	59	100

Cocoa is still, by far, the most important orchard crop and fewer farmers are growing alternative orchard crops than in the Atewa Range. Although cocoa was decimated by swollen shoot disease in the 1940s, new swollen-shoot resistant hybrid varieties have been planted. The New Suhum area has been a centre for the World Bank assisted Cocoa Rehabilitation Project and several farmers at Kofi Pare have received assistance and loans for planting new varieties of cocoa, purchasing inputs and hiring labour.

Cocoa is more important in Kofi Pare than in the Atewa Range, but fewer farmers have cocoa plantations. While between 60–80 percent of both men and women have cocoa plantations in the Atewa Range about 50 percent of men and 30 percent of women have plantations in Kofi Pare. There is almost a gender division of crops with fewer women planting cocoa and more women focussing on roots, tubers and vegetables. However, a large number of men under the age of 45 are also excluded from cocoa cultivation.

Table 2.9 *Estimated sizes of cocoa plantations*

Size of plantations	Male	Female	Total
2 acres and less	27	56	34
2–5 acres	31	22	29
5–20 acres	39	22	34
Over 20 acres	4		3
No. of farmers	26	9	35

Figure 2.4 *Distribution of mature cocoa plantations at Kofi Pare*

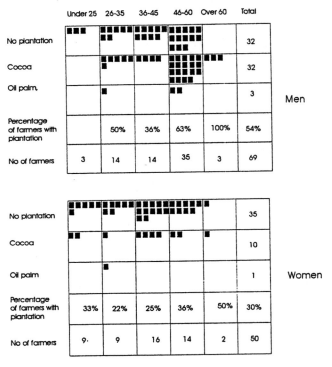

Figure 2.5 *Crops planted on new farms in the 1999/2000 season*

Kofi Pare

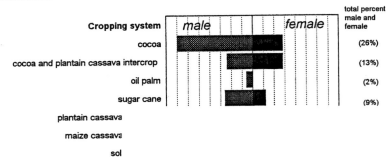

While fewer farmers have established plantations at Kofi Pare, the areas of cocoa plantations are larger than in the Atewa Range settlements. A large proportion of plantations owned by men are between 5–20 acres. Most women cocoa farmers have smaller plantations, although a smaller proportion than in the Atewa Range settlements have plantations of 2 acres and under. This suggests that there is less equitable distribution of agricultural assets and land at Kofi Pare. The access of a large number of farmers to land for plantation cultivation is being suppressed to maintain middle sized cocoa holdings that can be farmed profitably. This number includes a large number of women and youth farmers. Unfortunately, this tentative conclusion cannot be backed up with data on the size of land holdings that farmers have available. While many farmers can provide estimates of the size of their plantations, they are unable to provide accurate estimates of the total land they have available for food farming, which is often scattered in various localities.

Conclusion

There are similarities and differences in the economy of the two areas, which is a result of the larger regional economy in which the settlements are integrated and differences that arise from their different histories. In both settlements there is an increasingly mobile population, which reflects a declining dependence on agriculture. Many of the citizens of the two areas depend on incomes gained from work outside of family agricultural land. Many of the youth have alternative incomes to agriculture, including casual labour, small scale mining and work carrying timber boards. The latter two activities are more pronounced in the timber rich auriferous Atewa Range settlements. A large number of women combine farming with petty trading. A few artisans operate within the two settlements who have received training through an apprenticeship. They serve as carpenters, masons, dressmakers and hairdressers. However, the demand for their services is limited within the settlements and those that remain often combine their trade with farming. A large percentage of the youth population are highly mobile, seeking livelihood opportunities in towns and cities, moving between occasionally farming in their home town and working within the informal sector in cities and small towns. A large number of youth born to parents residing in these areas have left to seek work in towns and cities. The land of these settlements can no longer support those it gives birth to, and the children of the land no longer seek to reproduce themselves within the agricultural sector. This partially reflects declining profitability of cocoa production, as farmers are beset with low world market prices and growing costs in rehabilitating old plantations.

Access to land is another important factor and many youth migrate because they cannot gain sufficient land for farming purposes. Land is more constrained at Kofi Pare, where a significant proportion of youth and women can no longer gain access to family land to make a viable agricultural livelihood. This partially reflects historical circumstances. The cocoa industry at Kofi Pare was built on a few large cocoa farmers with large holdings and their dependants who they allocated small pieces of land in return for services. The large holdings have now been subdivided into smaller holdings farmed by the heirs who originally purchased the land, but these are retained as medium sized plantations which are transmitted to the next generation, rather than being further partitioned into smaller holdings. As a result of this women often get limited access to agricultural land. In contrast, there is a more equitable distribution of land on gender lines at Apinaman and Dwinease and participation of women in cocoa farming, although land pressures are building up. This reflects the participation of women in cocoa farming from its inception in the early decades of the twentieth century, and the transmission of women's family property to daughters and granddaughters.

Chapter 3
Land, Labour and Matrikin

In recent years a growing number of studies have advocated the empowerment of community based land tenure systems. However few of these studies actually provide empirical case studies of the management of land in communities in the contemporary period. Many of these studies are based on hypothetical models of how land was managed in traditional systems. They are usually vague about the specifics and dynamics of land management. Few of them actually refer to the lineage units in which land is managed. Land is rarely under community management in African societies, but under various lineages and lineage heads. These, rather than the community, comprise corporate agricultural landholding units in most societies. Although many recent studies on community participation in land management are inspired by anthropological approaches, they make scant reference to the anthropological literature on kinship, which contains considerable data on the lineage management of land. Moreover, they fail to take into account the large amount of literature generated in the 1960s and 1970s which examined the impact of social change on kinship organisation, community relations and agricultural production. This literature began to develop a historical dimension that critically questioned the ahistoricism and idealistic foundations of structural-functionalist anthropology; examined the impact of modernisation and social change on the organisation of lineages and the emergence of social differentiation and of entrepreneurs (Parkin, 1972; Barth, 1967; Hill, 1963; 1970); and developed a political economic dimension concerned with the incorporation of communities, peasants, and lineages into global systems of production, processes of social differentiation, crisis and transformation (Asad, 1979; Amin, 1972; Meillassoux, 1964; 1971; Dupré and Rey, 1978).

This chapter examines the role of the matrilineal system in land management in the two case study areas of Kofi Pari and the Atewa Range settlements. It examines the different modes through which different producers gain access to land; the perspectives of different categories of producers on the role of the matrilineage in the control and allocation of land; the relationship between matriliny, land allocation and the relations of production, and the relationship between agricultural production, matrilineal kinship and land administration.

Land and matriliny

Ideologies of kinship and descent inform the transmission of land from one generation to the next in the societies under consideration. However, these conceptions are themselves changing and being reinterpreted and become charged with new nuances as the economic and social conditions of life change. Various discourses on kinship and inheritance exist which relate to various subjective experiences of life. These are often fragmented. Rarely is a total abstracted picture produced of the kinship system in relation to inheritance of the type favoured by classic colonial anthropology, in the mould we of x culture subscribe to y values and in accordance with this carry out z actions. This kind of authoritative discourse could be reproduced when an anthropologist asks questions in the mode of what do *you* do in your culture, stressing their position as an ambassador of a foreign culture, and the discussion as a discourse on different cultures. In such a *tête à tête* the community in question would do his/her best to appease the anthropologist by electing a member of the community versed in authoritative discourse to be the ambassador of their culture, and this authority figure would do their best to give a totalising picture of their culture.

In contrast with authoritative discourse, folk discourses frequently deal with the daily relations between people in facing material life. They deal with issues of guile and greed, cunning, folly, betrayal, generosity, meanness, money, lack of money, work, no work, sickness, and production looms large.

The people of Apinaman and Dwenease, are classified as matrilineal. However, this does not mean that they consciously live out their life according to a specified code of matriliny or according to an essentialist Akan ideology or culture that is based on matriliny. As Asad (1979:621) writes:

> The problem of understanding ideology is therefore wrongly formulated when it is assumed to be a matter of predicting what 'real' or 'experiential' social forms are necessarily produced or reproduced by it. And this is so not because forms of utterance never have systematic consequences ... but because the effectiveness of such utterances is dependent on conventions which are viable only within particular material conditions.

Matriliny cannot be seen as an ideology that structures relations of production, reproduction, property and inheritance outside of the material conditions of society, since these very relations are what are constituted as matriliny. However, this is what pertains in much of the anthropological literature. This is very clearly illustrated by the concept of the matrilineal puzzle (Richards, 1950). Richards argues that the adoption of a matrilineal principle of social organisation results in a paradox which cannot be resolved. According to the matrilineal principle, inheritance and the administration of lineage property passes from the mother's brother to the sisters' sons. If the mother's brother remains in his house to carry out these functions, then his wife's children, who will have responsibility in his wife's matrilineage will be alienated from their matrilineal house. If he resides with his wife he will be away from his matrilineal house over which he exerts authority. In this analytic framework, people are seen as living life according to some ideological principle that produces unresolvable contradictions, instead of seeing matriliny as the outcome of social relations between different categories of people (defined by age, gender and economic wealth/independence, etc.), and the institutions for the control of household labour and control and transmission of property.

Several researchers have argued that matriliny declines with development and with increasing wealth and social differentiation (Goody, 1959; Murdock, 1949). They argue that with increasing social differentiation the redistribution of wealth along extended family networks tends to break down and men seek to invest their self-acquired wealth in their children. However, other studies have argued the opposite, that matriliny continues to survive and adapt to changing conditions (Fortes, 1950, 1969; Hill, 1963; Okali, 1983).

Mary Douglas (1969) has asserted that it is not differentiated wealth that causes rich men to favour their sons over their sister's sons as much as scarcity in resources. She argues that the major characteristics of matriliny are an open texture of recruitment to descent groups (vague rules of inclusion and exclusion) and a tendency towards wide ranging recruitment of manpower. This enables flexible patterns of social organisation and succession, with emphasis on achievement rather than ascription. Enterprising men can mobilise their matrilineal kin around their economic and political strategies to further their ambitions and build up the wealth and prestige of the matrilineage in the process. She argues that matriliny is well adapted to any situation in which competing demands for men are higher than demands for resources, such as where land is plentiful and labour scarce:

> In poor agrarian systems, such as those of traditional matrilineal regions across the centre of Africa, a man's labour is more valuable than any fixed capital: land is generally plentiful, labour is scarce. One of the problems a community in such a region must solve is how to recruit new blood and maintain its manpower at the necessary level of skills and energy. I have argued that matrilineal institutions serve this end. Flexibility of association is an advantage in communities most denuded of material wealth, where the value of material goods is much less than the value of persons (Douglas, 1969:130).

Douglas argues that matriliny will continue to survive where the labour of people continues to be valued more than fixed capital. With economic expansion, matriliny can flourish where the demand for men is higher than for things, and that its open texture recruitment can encourage the formation of effective economic corporate organisations with leadership chosen from the most talented members. She cites the matrilineal family lands of migrant cocoa farmers in southern Ghana, as described by Hill (1963) as an example of modern corporations based on matriliny. Douglas argues that in periods of recession and resource scarcity the matrilineal principles will be under threat: "Competition in a restricted field causes men to draw in their horns and to concentrate their responsibilities on their nearest kin" (1963:130).

In her analysis Douglas only focuses on successful men and their relations to matrilineal property and political control of property. She does not examine the perspective of poorer men, women and youth. She fails to examine the different social relations in families and lineages that contribute to the constitution of matriliny.

In contrast, Fortes (1969) looks at matriliny among the Asante in the context of various social relations between men and women through three generational levels, from the grandparent sibling level to their grandchildren. Fortes (1969:206) comments on the responsibilities of men towards their own and their sisters' children:

> He has the avuncular duty to help his sisters to equip their children for adult life too, especially if (as can happen in the circumstances of Ashanti family structure) by reason of divorce, or lack of means, or some other impediment, the children's fathers are negligent.

In his survey of 500 ever-married women in Ashanti in 1945, 43 percent were divorced or widowed, and of the 57 percent still married approximately 1 in 4 were living with children without any regular support from their husbands. In contrast with the assertion of Douglas, it appears here that inability to support one's own children and insecurity of marriage are also factors encouraging matriliny, or at least matrifocality.

Matrifocality refers to female centred kinship relations, which are usually based on mother's mother, mother and children (Smith, 1996; 1973). Instability of marriage and inability of men to take responsibility for children as a result of economic difficulty, results in domestic units that consist of two generations of women and children—mother's mother, mother and children (Smith, 1996, 1973; Fayorsey, 1995).

Although theories of matrifocality have not been constructed in matrilineal societies, matriliny can be seen to embody an extension of matrifocality through the bond of siblings. While the classic matrifocal situation consists of an economic and social alliance between mother, daughters and grandchildren, matriliny involves an alliance between mother, children and grandchildren, in which the sons takes responsibility for their sisters' children.

The theoretical significance of the literature on matrifocality is that it draws a clear distinction between ideal constructs of kinship systems and the statistical norms. The arrangements of living in a material world are often different from ideological constructs of authentic culture. The ideals are often the ideological constructs of dominant elite interests in society. Since kinship analysis and social systems have often been approached through the values of the dominant male household heads, ideological representations of a kinship system have been manifested as the actual working of the system. This does not mean that ideational systems are not important. As Smith (1996) shows, while matrifocal families are statistically dominant in Guyana, most people at some time in their life pass through a conjugal nuclear family, and aspire to live as a married nuclear couple, although that union may in the long term be fragile.

The literature on matrifocality is important in that it challenges evolutionary schemes that posit the nuclear patrifocal (male headed) family as the final developed and evolved form of the family in the golden age of mature capitalism. From this, it is evident that the options open for the evolution of societies characterised as matrilineal do not consist only of the replacement of matrilineal "open texture" lineages by patrifocal nuclear families, or the successful integration of matrilineages as entrepreneurial corporate groups under the chairmanship of enterprising mothers' brothers (the position of Mary Douglas). Matrilineages can also be transformed into various matrifocal units, in which the authority and responsibility of men as husbands and as brothers of women become eroded by economic insecurity and social turmoil, ushered in by the expansion of global market ideologies and practices. This can occur without any transformation of ideologies of kinship—just as matrifocality occurs in societies in which the dominant interests espouse patrilineal values. Thus, if matrilineal principles are breaking down or being transformed, the transformation is not necessarily from the commanding position of the mother's brother to the father, it can also involve the emergence of networks of women based around economic production and social and domestic reproduction.

Okali (1983) challenges the view that the matrilineal principle is breaking down as a result of husbands attempting to leave their farms to their children in contemporary economic settings. She argues that it is rather wives, who are demanding that the services they perform in farm work are reciprocated and "if none are given and they felt they have alternatives, divorce would ensue" (1983:145–146). Okali examines matriliny within the cocoa economy in terms of the specific investments in farms, including labour and service, and the interests and expectations of different types of relatives, including wives, sons and nephews of farm owners.

Patrifocal relations have been important in Akan society for a long period of time. Joint economic relations between fathers and sons are not a modern phenomenon. In a fascinating account of the Akani trading organisations in the seventeenth century, Kea (1982) shows the importance of patrifocal relations in Akan society. Throughout the seventeenth century, the Akani merchants of Assin were recognised to be the most successful traders in the hinterland of the Gold Coast and sold as much as two-thirds of the gold European trading companies exported. Their trading organisations were organised over a large area extending from the coastal towns west of Accra into the Adanse, Kwabre and Akyem areas. They mediated exchange between fishing, salt producing and gold producing areas, and enjoyed a near monopoly over the circulation of goods within the interior. The Akani trading organisation came under the direct control of the Assin nobility and functioned as a state administered economic enterprise. The nobility sponsored and organised trading caravans. The trading organisation was an integral part of state structure and was controlled by the state council. The trading organisations were corporate organisations under captains. These captains came under the jurisdiction of hereditary political stools. The trading associations were organised as a merchants' guild with master brokers, brokers and apprentices. Specialised mercantile knowledge in these guilds was transmitted from senior men to their younger brothers and their sons. Sons and younger brothers succeeded fathers and elder brothers. However, these merchant-brokers inherited property from within their matrilineages. Thus, a successful mercantile organisation would have been able to utilise the property of a number of matrilineages in their trading operations and to draw upon the services of a large number of individuals recruited from different matrilineages. The Akani trading organisations would have been able to use the capital of these matrilineages as working or venture capital.

The corollary of men who are unable to look after their children and their sisters' children as a result of economic insecurity or poverty, are successful individuals who are able to mobilise sons, younger brothers, brothers' children, and matrilineal kin (all of whom are looking for successful kin to help them achieve a livelihood) to build up large economic ventures. A synergism exists between both situations, since the first enables the second to come into being. Thus, one should not look to one particular evolutionary path for the domestic family and its economy under matriliny. A plurality of hybrid arrangements can exist reflecting different life and material circumstances, including prosperous men who are able to mobilise a large number of matrilineal relatives, sons and younger brothers; poor men unable to support children or sisters' children; and matrifocal units without benevolent male benefactors.

The problem with a large body of literature on matriliny, land and social transformation, is that it represents authentic matriliny as the discourse of dominant and economically successful men. The challenge in examining the domestic household or family economy, is to represent the various clashes of interests and the ideological discourses that arise, and the transformation of the discourses in the light of changing material conditions of life.

An essentialist theoretical framework reduces the problem of social change to a struggle between different cultural systems and ideational principles. This concept of social change is usually rooted in one epoch which is deemed as having paramount significance by the social scientist, whether on the eve of colonial conquest, as for the early colonial anthropologists of Malinoski's generation, the post-independence period for post-structural-functionalist anthropologists (transactionists and structuralists), and the "era of globalisation" for post-modernists. This prime epoch of change is seen as breaking down authentic tradition. However, this paradigm results in theoretical inconsistencies. If all societies have had histories that precede colonialism and globalisation and culture is a product of these histories, how have these histories interacted with authentic essential tradition? And since humans can only think surrounded by material life, how have these essentialist cultural ideational principles come into being to organise the whole of material life and people's conception of material life? Thus, the problem of social change cannot be reduced to an understanding of a decline of broad ideational cultural principles in the face of growing commodification or westernisation. Matriliny cannot be seen as an ideational principle that stands in opposition to social change, commodification, capitalism, westernisation or globalisation which must perish as these expand.

'The relations of production and reproduction construed as matriliny need to be analysed within specific material conditions, and changing material conditions. They need to be seen as arising from the relationship of specific categories of people who come to constitute families and households, and as the product of the changing economic conditions that mediate and structure these social relations. In different epochs what is construed as the principles of inheritance, descent and household administration will change in accordance with changing conditions of material life, without necessarily resulting in any major struggle of ideas over the definition of kinship or lineage. Around these changing material conditions different discourses will emerge, seeking to establish meaning and to interpret, re-interpret, justify or condemn the direction of change. These positions will reflect different political and economic interests.

Principles of land tenure and circuits of access to land

In the following analysis the relations governing access to land and the land tenure system are not deduced from a set of ideational principles rooted in the ideology of lineage or cultural perceptions. They are not viewed as a product of these underlying principles or the transformation of these principles by processes of commodification, modernisation, westernisation or social change. They are elicited by building a description of the different circuits through which people gain land.

In the Akyem areas access to land can be gained through seven basic circuits:

1. Through clearing mature forest land which has not been cultivated for a long period;
2. Inheritance through matrilineal kin;
3. A gift of land from a relative;
4. The loan of land by a relative, affine or friend;
5. Land purchase;
6. Through crop share arrangements;
7. Land leasing.

Land clearance

In the early part of the twentieth century citizens could gain rights in land through clearing mature forest land. Danquah (1928b:xxx) states:

> Any person born of Akyem Abuakwa parents being a member of an Akyem Abuakwa clan has inalienable right to cultivate a Stool land unsold or uncultivated or unreserved; and whilst that person occupies a farm thus made, the particular piece of uncultivated forest land appurtenant to his farm and about the same size as his old farm (one season's or year's cultivation) is presumed by law to be appropriated by him; that is to say the forest land adjoining his farm is regarded as his forest land reserved for his cultivation ...

This principle is vividly illustrated by Field's informants in Akyem Kotoku:

> Wherever your cutlass has touched is yours and your children's for ever. When you tire of clearing new forest you can come back to the old. Children come back to where their grandfather cleared.

'My own farm is in the *kwae* called *Ahomamu*, and so are my sons' farms. I am father of Ahomamu [i.e. one of the original farmers in this forest area]. I have a boundary with Yao Odonko on my right and with Yao Duke on my left. The old path is behind me: I started from there. In front I am still advancing, and I can clear in front till I reach the stream Nyenesu. You always go on clearing in front of you till you reach a river, somebody's old farm, or a path. You may cross a path if you like, but you often make a path your boundary. But you must never cross a stream.'

A young man, Kwami Dakwa, gave me an account of his food farm and of food farming generally.

'My farm', he said, 'is in the *kwae* called *Kanyiso*. My father began cultivating there. Three other people started abreast of him, but also worked towards the stream. These were:

'Kodzo Ansa, my father's younger brother.
'Kwesi Edin, my father's brother-in-law.
'Kweku Sei, my father's brother-in-law.

'We like to work abreast, because if you have nothing but forest round your farm wild animals are always spoiling your crops.

'All four of these people worked towards Esu Kese. Later my father gave my brother Donko and me plots on his farm between him and the stream. Donko works towards the stream and I work towards Donko. When I meet him I shall turn West into my father's land. It is all my father's on the West until someone else meets him there, but no one has yet come. If a newcomer came he would start farther West against the path and work towards the stream. He could work towards the East if he liked, but if my father wanted to stop him he could do so by clearing a small farm against the path of his advance.

'My farm is cleared down to the boundary between me and my brother Donko. It is now a food farm. When it has finished growing food I shall plant cocoa there and make a new farm somewhere else for food. I think I shall clear towards the West into my father's land, but if I like I can ask my uncle to give me some of his land. Perhaps he will give me land already cleared but perhaps not cleared. Or if I like I could start in a new *kwae* altogether. There is still some unallocated *kwae* and if you are not a stranger you can take it without asking the chief. If somebody else has already taken it he must show me, in proof, the beginning of his cultivation if he wants to keep me out' (Field,1948:66–69)

The early twentieth century was a period of major forest clearance in the forest zone of Ghana, in which large areas of frontier forests were converted into cocoa farms. Among citizens, rights in land were largely acquired by organising labour for forest clearance. Today the situation is different. Few areas of uncultivated mature forest exist, and rights to lands are rarely acquired by moving into uncultivated forest areas. Farmers are now largely dependent upon transfers of land from kin or on market transactions of land such as purchase, renting or sharecropping.

Kinship relations and land

The Akan matrilineage (*abusua*) has been defined by Fortes (1969) as a maximal lineage consisting of the uterine descendants of a common ancestress of three generations. This consists of the siblings of the mother's mother's generation and the children and grandchildren of the women. This unit is defined as a corporate group by it having an *abusuafie* (matrilineal house) with a blackened stool and a deity and an *abusuapanin* (male family elder) and an *obaapanin* (female family elder). *Abusua* members have joint responsibilities to organise and finance the funeral of all of their members. The family property is administered by the *abusuapanin*. Succession to the office of *abusuapanin* is transmitted through the line of senior mother's brother to junior mother's brother and from the line of mother's brother to that of mother's son.

While the family property is administered by the *abusuapanin*, individual members of the *abusua* have rights to use parts of the family property. Properties that *abusua* members create in their own lifetime are recognised as individual properties. Parts of this property can be transmitted to wives and offspring in the life of the owner through gifts, or by deathbed declarations. Gifts of property are formally made with witnesses from the lineage. In front of the elders of the *abusua* the giver of the land pronounces that he/she is making a gift of property to the recipient. The gift is sealed by the recipient providing *aseda* (thank you), which currently usually takes the form of some drink (schnapps), a sheep, and some money. This seals the transference of the property. This gift is usually made by a man to his male and female children and the children of his sisters. Women can also gift property to their children. Danquah (1928a) writes that the successor to a woman's property is usually a female relative.

Gifts of land can also be made by husbands to wives. In the early part of the twentieth century one of Field's (1948:69) informants stated:

> A husband may give his wife a farm for herself and then the profits are hers entirely, but when he gives her the farm she must give him rum [*aseda*] before witnesses as a sign that the farm is now hers. Then, even if there is a divorce, the farm remains hers. But if there is no rum put on the gift the farm is the husband's to farm and it stays with him if there is a divorce.

Field (1948:72) comments that the heirs of men are:

> ... usually nephews belonging to his own *abusua*, but he can and is expected to give cleared lands to his sons, daughters and wife. Such gifts must be sealed with rum in the presence of witnesses, and then remain the property of the recipients and their successors or legatees.

While Danquah (1928a) recognises the gift of land to both children and matrilineal relatives as common in Akyem Abuakwa in the early twentieth century, he suggests that this is partly the result of acculturation and the adoption of Christianity:

> In Akim Abuakwa the erstwhile Basel Mission Society—the only missionary society which has successfully operated in the Akim dominions—has evolved a form of succession for the benefit of its Christian communities. This form of succession, which seems to have obtained favour among the Christians, is shortly as follows;—when a member of the Basel (now Scottish) Mission Domination dies, his property would be divided into three—one-third goes to the wife, the second third to the children, and the remaining third to the [matrilineal] relatives of the deceased. ... This role, which has taken a strong hold on the minds of the Christian converts—a rapidly increasing community—has also affected other distinct changes among the general mass of the people. A rich man, for instance, would in these days of economic agriculture, provide well for his children by apportioning them in his lifetime substantial parts of his property. The act is done in the presence of the family, but their assent is not required by law. The transfer would then be for ever. When drink is given in testimony and an "Aseda" taken, the gift bears legal examination in the Tribunals. It is not denied that there must have been some indigenous basis for this practice which led to the establishment of the missionary procedure in the country, but when we remember that there was very little of the individualistic ownership of property before the missionary and the trader went to Africa, it can easily be seen that modern tendencies have much to do with the changes brought about by the contact of Europe and West Africa (Danquah, 1928a:185).

Danquah probably exaggerates the role of Christianity in bringing about these changes, but he is right in pointing out the considerable changes brought about by the development of cocoa farming in the commodification of land and labour. The whole basis of family labour on farms and inheritance of land was transformed by these developments. They were also transformed by the abolishment of domestic slavery. Land and the products of labour gained a new valorisation that they did not have before. Thus "traditional" inheritance or authentic kinship cultural patterns cannot be deduced from examining the operation of kinship in the cocoa economy at the turn of the century.

Data collected by Polly Hill on the early matrilineal migrant cocoa farmers of Akuapem, operating in the Densu valley, shows a clear alliance between fathers, sons and matrikin in the development of oil palm farming in the mid-nineteenth century and the reinvestment of profits in cocoa. This prompted Hill (1963:84–85) to comment "some Akropong farmers pay so much regard to the rights of their sons that it would seem almost appropriate to regard them as subject to a dual inheritance system". Hill (1963) also noted that cocoa lands purchased by matrilineal cocoa farmers have not become more patrilineal over time, but have maintained a uniquely matrilineal structure of inheritance:

> At that time [about sixty years ago] an investigator might well have forecast the immanent collapse, as a result of the development of commercial cocoa-farming, of the Aburi 'matrilineal system', partly on general grounds and partly because prominent Christian farmers, ministers, catechists and others who were, of course, concerned to provide for their sons, were so much in evidence as purchasers of trans-Densu lands. Today no such prognostication can be ventured, it having meanwhile become apparent that the family land system is a form of matrilineal organization which has not merely survived intact but has also proved its strength (1963:81–82).

It seems unlikely that the importance of sons in cocoa farming can be attributed merely to acculturation and the adoption of Christianity. It must be rooted in the dynamics of farm management and labour arrangements.

Okali (1983) focuses on the problem of property rights within the family in relation to the acquisition and development of farms, the distribution of returns and the transfer of farms from one generation to the next. She examines conflicts between husbands and wives, fathers and sons and mothers' brothers and sisters' sons in this context. She argues that successful cocoa farmers supplement hired labour with the labour of relatives, and recruit this from wives, children and matrilineal kin. These kin work on an understanding that as the enterprise flourishes they will be rewarded in future with gifts of cocoa plantations, which they have been instrumental in creating through their labour and supervision of hired labour. This involves extended reciprocity over a long period, since it takes considerable time for cocoa plantations to become well-established profit making ventures and for the arrangements that cocoa farmers make for the future of their dependants and wives to come to fruition. Frequently, cocoa farmers die before their farm investments have matured. This often results in bitter disputes between wives, children and matrikin over rights to cocoa plantations. In this process, those who have expended considerable efforts on making farms for their seniors may be bitterly disappointed, as the fruits of their labour are usurped by matrilineal heirs, such as junior brothers, who may not have contributed to the farm enterprise. Okali (1983:107) reports of one son, who had managed his father's cocoa farms only to be displaced by his father's heir. The son bitterly declared: "If you follow your father you are a fool for nothing". In other instances, dependants may withdraw their service from their senior (their father or uncle), when they see other relatives are being treated more favourably than themselves, or better opportunities exist elsewhere with other relatives:

> Once his father had failed to provide for his future and an alternative was offered there was no question of his staying at Dominase (Okali, 1983:106).

The same situation can occur to sisters' children, who may also find themselves displaced by the junior brothers of their mother's senior brother.

This contrasts with the situation reported by Field for the early part of the century, in which men provided gifts of land for youths and wives to set them up in life:

> My father was a hunter and didn't trouble himself about farms. Our fathers never did. But nowadays we have begun giving farms to our sons. I have two sons and I gave each of them a farm when he was about fifteen. My daughter too was about sixteen when I gave her a farm of her own. Before that the boys helped me and the girl helped her mother (Field, 1948:66).

> A father also gives his daughters farms so they can work and buy cloth and things for themselves. The mother comes and thanks the father with rum when he gives the daughter a farm. The daughter plants food crops in her new farm and when the food-growing power dies the father comes and plants cocoa for her and gives her a new food farm elsewhere. When she marries, her father will say to the husband, "I have given your wife this farm. When the food crops finish come and plant cocoa for her and it will be hers". If she is a hard-working girl and plants cocoa for herself before her marriage, the cocoa profits are hers though she may be still unmarried (Field, 1948:70–71).

While this may be a slightly idealised picture (which is based on narration by an informant rather than on statistical patterns), there are significant differences between life in the early twentieth and later twentieth century that have implications for the gift of land. The narratives of Field's informants take place in a period of cocoa boom when a large supply of frontier land existed. Rights to land could be established through clearing mature forest and this became the individual property of farmers which could be disposed of as they pleased. In contrast, Okali's narrative occurs in the 1970s, a period of recession and growing land shortage as frontier land becomes scarce. Competition for land produces conflicts over ownership, and the slow process of capital accumulation in recession, results in the situation where enterprising men may die before they have established their own personal estate and allocated rights to their dependants. With growing land scarcity, gifts become increasingly contentious and open to dispute between matrilineal members and between matrilineal members and children.

User rights in land

In place of giving land as a gift to a family member land may be allocated to a relative or close friend to "eat from" or to cultivate freely. Men may give land to children or sisters' children and wives on this basis. Women may give land to their children and grandchildren on this arrangement. Women also can give land to spouses on this basis. Okali (1983) found that this was a common arrangement at Akokoaso between citizen women and their migrant husbands.

Gaining user rights in land is often the first stage which children pass through before they are given a gift of the plot. If children cannot afford to make the *aseda* payment to seal the granting of land as a gift, they will hold land on a user right basis. Frequently children start off working with their father or mother on their farms, and then are given a plot of their own on which to make a farm, before this plot is later formally presented to them as a gift.

Sharecrop arrangements

In the past sharecrop arrangements were mainly transacted between migrant farmers and citizen landowners. However, as land has become increasingly scarce, few youth have the option of clearing uncultivated forest land to create their own farms and many of them are obliged to seek sharecrop land to supplement the land they can gain from their families. Sharecrop land is usually given on the basis of the landlord taking a third share of the produce and the tenant two-thirds (*abusa*), or a half share (*abunu*). The *abunu* arrangement is displacing the older *abusa* system, which was more common in the period 1920–1960. Sometimes some of the crops grown are shared on *abunu* and others on *abusa* agreements.

Land leasing

Hiring of land for monetary payment is not very common in the forest zone and land is usually leased on the basis of the *abunu* or *abusa* system. Where land is hired it is usually for short season vegetable farming, such as garden eggs, okra and tomatoes.

Purchase of land

In the past land purchase by citizens was rare since citizens could acquire land by clearing mature forest. Land purchase was common by migrant farmers, who usually purchased uncultivated mature forest land from stools rather than individuals. With growing shortage of land and demand for land, the potential for an internal land market to develop within settlements exists. However, it is difficult for individuals to sell family land, since there are multiple interests in this land. The sale of family land usually has to be justified by an urgent need to raise money to pay for land litigation and court cases, to settle family debts, and to pay for medical treatment for a family member, etc.

Land in the Atewa Range settlements

In contemporary Apinaman and Dwenease, there are four main methods through which farmers gain access to land. The dominant method is through kinship and marriage ties. Sharecropping is also important. A number of men also purchase land. The fourth circuit involves illicitly clearing and farming forest reserve land—a desperate measure.

Table 3.1 *Sources of land farmed at Apinaman and Dwenease*

Source of land	Apinaman			Dwenease		
	Male	Female	Total	Male	Female	Total
Purchase	12	.	6	7	.	4
Cleared from *kwae* (forested) land	.	.	.	14	.	10
Sharecrop	19	.	11	34	5	23
Mother	4	41	21	14	32	22
Mother's mother	8	18	13	.	11	4
Mother's brother	15	5	10	10	.	7
Maternal grand uncle	4	.	2	.	.	.
Father	4	.	2	27	32	29
Father's father	4	.	2	.	5	4
Father's mother	15	.	8	3	5	4
Paternal great grandfather	.	5	2	.	.	.
Spouse	19	5	14	14	.	8
Spouse's mother	4	5	4	.	.	.
Clearing Forest Reserve	.	5	2	3	.	2
None	4	19	10	.	21	8
No. of respondents	26	24	50	29	19	48

In the survey, mother's brothers do not play a dominant role in the transfer of land from one generation to the next. Only 10 percent of the respondents at Apinaman and 7 percent at Dwenease received land from their mother's brother. But neither can fathers be said to be the dominant land providers, at least for Apinaman. At Apinaman only 2 percent of respondents received land from their fathers. At Dwenease 29 percent of the farmers received land from their fathers, but only 15 percent of farmers were dependent on their fathers alone for land and the other 14 percent supplemented land from their father with land from mothers, other relatives, or from sharecropping. This suggests that small portions of land were being allocated by fathers. Fifteen percent of women received land from both father and mother. Male children receiving land from their father did not gain any from their mothers. A larger proportion of women at Dwenease gained land from their father than men.

In both settlements mothers and mother's mothers play an important role in transferring land to the next generation. At Apinaman 34 percent of farm land had been transferred to the present farmer by their mothers or mother's mothers. 59 percent of women received land from their mother or mother's mother, but only 12 percent of men received their land through mothers and their mother's mother. At Dwenease 26 percent of farm plots had been transmitted to the present farmers by mothers and mother's mothers, including 43 percent of women and only 14 percent of men.

A third discernible pattern of access to land is through spouses. The most significant pattern here is not women working on their husband's land, but men working on their wives' and wives' mothers land. At Dwenease 14 percent of men were farming on land that belonged to their spouse and at Apinaman 23 percent of men worked on land belonging to their wife or wife's mother.

A fourth pattern involves farmers receiving land from relatives in the grandparent generation rather than from their parents (father, mother, mother's brother) generation. This is particularly pronounced at Apinaman where 27 percent of farmers gained their land from the grandparent generation rather than their parents as compared with 12 percent of farmers at Dwenease. At Apinaman 31 percent of men gained their land from the grandparent generation as compared to 23 percent of women. While women mainly gained land from the grandparent generation through their mother's mother, the most significant category for men was their father's mother. Thus, at Apinaman, the role of fathers in providing land for their sons has been usurped by their mothers.

A fifth significant pattern is the large number of men who gain access to land outside of kinship obligations, through market or contractual relations. 19 percent of farmers at Apinaman, and 39 percent at Dwenease use land that has been gained either through purchase, sharecropping or clearing of forest land. These non-kinship circuits are more prevalent among men than women: 58 percent of men at Dwenease and 31 percent at Apinaman gain land through non-kinship relations as compared to five percent of women in both settlements. Sharecropping and illegal clearing of land are more prevalent at Dwenease than Apinaman. 34 percent of farmers use sharecropping land at Dwenease as compared to 19 percent at Apinaman. In both settlements a few men gain access to land through purchase. At Apinaman 12 percent of men in the sample made farms on land they have purchased as compared to 7 percent of Dwenease men. Another mode of access—which many people would not admit in a survey—is through illicitly clearing land in the forest reserve.

Land shortage is perceived to be more prevalent at Dwenease than at Apinaman. Most farmers are unable to provide accurate estimates on the size of their landholding (and it was beyond the scope of the research to measure plots). Nevertheless, 43 percent of farmers at Dwenease felt they suffered from land shortage as compared to 73 percent at Dwenease. At Apinaman 48 percent of male and 38 percent of female respondents felt they had insufficient land for farming as compared to 90 percent of men and 47 percent of women at Dwenease. This intense shortage of land at Dwenease accounts for the large number of people gaining land through non-kinship circuits.

Land shortage and declining male authority

In the past matrilineages were organised around powerful men—the *abusuapanin* of the lineages. The most successful of these men recruited a support base from among their children, their nephews and their junior brothers. Young men would render services to them or serve a long apprenticeship learning a craft. At the end of this they would be rewarded with access to property and a livelihood. By the early twentieth century enterprising men began to move into agriculture and cocoa as a field of investment. Before this period, in the Akyem area food crop farming was considered the main preserve of women. Gold mining was an important economic activity prior to colonialism. During the colonial period small-scale gold mining became depressed as a result of the strictures of colonial rule which banned small-scale mining (although it still continued), and the granting of concessions to expatriate firms. By the early twentieth century cocoa replaced gold mining as the major industry in the area and a period of rapid land clearance began. Men opened new *kwae* for cultivation and their sons and nephews helped them establish cocoa farms and were eventually rewarded for their service by the gift of cocoa plantations. Men also established farms for their daughters and wives. Family labour could be supplemented by hired labour which could be recruited from the large numbers of migrants from the savannah and Sahelian zones who came south. However, most cocoa farms established by Akyem citizens were small and depended more upon family than migrant hired labour (Beckett, 1947; Field, 1948; Hill, 1963).

During the early years of the cocoa boom migrant cocoa farmers also moved into the Akyem area purchasing large tracts of land from chiefs. One of the concerns of Dwenease citizens is that Apinaman chiefs alienated a large area of land to migrant farmers which they claim was their land. In the Atewa Range area, with encouragement from the colonial government, the *Okyenhene* also alienated a large area of land as forest reserve. The Atewa Range Forest Reserve was constituted in January 1926. The forest reserve was not created in pristine forest but encompassed farm land. The 1930–31 Forestry Department Annual Report comments:

> The political situation has not permitted the demarcation of either the Asamankese portion of the Atewa Range Reserve or of the Akwapim Hills Reserve. It is now eight years since these reserves were first proposed. Since then alienation in one and farming in the other have continued unchecked. It appears to be the case that unless forest land it is essential to conserve is brought under the protection of the Forest Ordinance as soon as it is so declared, the local inhabitants will at once start to clear the forest on it, frequently with no intention of farming it immediately but chiefly to prove that they have a right to farm there, or they will sell land in the area to strangers so that they themselves will not be saddled with any restrictions which may be put on it (pp. 3–4).

The 1930–31 Forestry Department Report also comments that in the Atewa Range Forest Reserve Administration Plan " 1–9 square miles of farmland are excluded from the operation of the [forest reserve] bye-laws" and that "controlled farming is admitted in suitable areas" (p. 6). Because of problems of administering this forest reserve with its mosaic of farm holdings, the reserve had to be reconstituted in 1935. The demarcation of the forest reserve was based largely on criteria related to watersheds rather than on land use patterns. They did not take into consideration fallow land not then being utilised and the future needs of communities for farming land.

As a result of land speculation and the alienation of land to migrant farmers and to the Forestry Department, a situation of artificially created land shortage has been superimposed on a process of rapid frontier expansion into low populated frontier districts by farming communities. This has resulted in a land shortage problem that is generationally structured. The first generation of cocoa farmers of the 1920s–1940s could establish ownership over large tracts of forest land which became individual property through clearance. The next generation met growing land shortage and had limited potential to clear new forest land. This generation had smaller lands and also limited access to land they could claim to have been created by their own labour, individual property that they had added to *abusua* property. They became more dependent upon *abusua* land and gifts from their fathers and matrilineal kin. The third generation has hardly any scope to clear its own land from forest land, and is competing with the second generation to use existing farm land.

While the first generation of cocoa farmers established their cocoa in a period of boom, the second generation met crisis in the cocoa economy. This crisis was manifest in the swollen shoot disease that decimated cocoa in the Eastern Region in the 1940s. Rehabilitation of cocoa land is expensive, involving the purchase of new hybrid varieties, and inputs that they require for successful cultivation. Rehabilitation of cocoa in old fallow land requires heavy expenditures of labour on weeding, since nefarious pan-tropical weeds, such as *Chromolaena odorata*, now dominate secondary forest and fallow land.

Hired farm labour has become scarce and expensive. The cheap migrant labour from the Sahel, which formed the backbone of the cocoa industry from the 1920s to the 1960s, has left Ghana for Côte d'Ivoire, following the imposition of policies hostile to migrants in the late 1960s and early 1970s, and the welcoming of migrants into the booming cocoa economy of the Côte d'Ivoire in the 1970s and 1980s (Amanor, 1998). Migrant labour within Ghana prefers to migrate to the new frontier districts of the Western Region and Ahafo rather than work in the declining cocoa areas of the Eastern Region. For the majority of farmers the high costs of labour are difficult to meet, particularly in these times of recession and high inflation. Cocoa farmers no longer reap the large profits they gained in the early twentieth century.

The booming cocoa economy of the 1920s and frontier expansion were translated into rapid population growth. During the nineteenth century the population of Akyem Abuakwa had been low. Large numbers of children were valued and provided labour for further frontier expansion, and security in old age. The demographic profile of the matrilineage was transformed by increasing numbers of young people. Men now became responsible for a large number of children and sisters' children. The expectations of these children also developed, and now men were not only expected to provide land for them and an apprenticeship in farming, but schooling and health care provisions. The deep recession of the 1970s and the structural adjustment response of the 1980s have brought about a crisis in family support mechanisms. The costs of production have increased as subsidies on inputs have been removed. Farmgate prices for food stuffs do not necessarily reflect increased costs of production, since trading monopolies over access to transport and to market places result in traders being able to establish monopoly prices. Declining urban living standards also create downward pressures on food prices. Social welfare provisioning has also been dismantled. School fees have to be paid, and school children are now expected to provide their own desks and exercise books. Health care is now subject to a cash and carry system in which even accident victims in critical condition have been refused treatment until they have provided the cost of treatment up front.

The decline of extended kinship welfare support

The increasing hardship and meanness of the state brought about by re-structuring to fit the requisites of globalisation affect kin relations. As one woman in her forties at Apinaman commented: "There is no *abusua* [ex-tended matrilineal family] nowadays because no brother or sister will help you. They will not even give you their leftover food". Another middle aged woman at Apinaman commented: "In the past when people had money they used to have good family ties. Now there is no money around and even if your *abusua* member loves you, you will not know [i.e. they cannot afford to express affection through material support and gifts]". A decline in recip-rocating ties between one generation of siblings will naturally be translated into a decline in the relationship with the children of one's siblings—if you can not share your food with your sister are you going to share it with your sister's children? As one woman in her late twenties at Apinaman said: "There is no *abusua*, because of hardship. After all, if I get something small I have to use it to feed myself. I cannot afford to feed my nephews".

The relationship between mother's brothers and sisters' sons deteriorate in this lean world. One sister's son commented on his mother's brother:

> "If I look at how I am suffering I believe there is no family system again. My uncle is overseas. He could have helped me but does not do anything for me. If I were his child he would have helped me"

This is a typical sentiment among nephews with poor or absent fathers. One elderly mother's brother at Apinaman also commented:

> "The *abusua* system is not working anymore. Now we work without children. Our nephews are now against us and they are even trying to kill us because they cannot get anything from us".[11]

Mature men now find it increasingly difficult to meet their obligations to-wards their children and their sisters' children. The majority of them do not have sufficient land to provide for the farming needs of these dependants. They do not have the financial means to provide for the welfare, education, food and clothing of their dependants. This growing inability of men to

---

[11] The theme of antagonism between sisters' sons and mother's brothers is an old theme in Akan society (see Fortes, 1969). What is new here, is the way that this is woven into a situation of changing allegiance in favour of children.

provide for the next generation results in a breakdown in the reciprocal relations of labour service provided by youth and provisioning of food, welfare and land by men. As one old man at Apinaman commented: "Elders don't have the strength to work and if you don't have money the youth see you to be a fool and won't help you". Box 3.1 records various perspectives on the relationship between youth and their senior kin in the present era.

Box 3.1
Because the world is hard: perceptions of declining family support for youth

"Because the world is hard now I have no money to give my children so wherever they pass they have to fend for themselves" (female, age 25–35).

"Because there is no money around, the parent of the youth cannot help them so everyone does as they please" (male, age 35–45, Dwenease).

"Because the family cannot take care of the youth they refuse to go to farm with their elders" (male, age 35–45, Apinaman).

"Because the elders no longer feed the youth everyone does as they please" (female, age 21–25, Apinaman).

"If you, a boy, ask your parents for school fees and they refuse you, you may have to work by-day [casual farm labour] to get the fees. The next time your parents call you [to do something for them] you may refuse to attend their call" (male, age 21–25, Dwenease).

The breakdown of the *abusua* is related to the increasing inability of its *abusuapanin* to manage the affairs of his kinsmen. In richer families extended kinship relations may still operate. As one old man at Dwenease stated:

The *abusua* still exists but its effectiveness depends on the *abusuapanin* and how he can organise the family. But because of high birth rate we are now moving over to our children.

This inability of senior men to provide for the needs of the junior members of the *abusua*, leads to the breakdown of generalised reciprocal ties of material support for juniors in return for labour service. This leads to perceptions of the breakdown of the *abusua*, reflected in declining mutual assistance, and a narrowing of those who one will help. While some people perceive this as a narrowing of mutual help to wife and children, others perceive it as a narrowing of interest to the individual, in which parents do not even support their own children. Box 3.2 echoes perceptions of the decline of the *abusua*.

Box 3.2

The abusua is collapsing: perspectives on declining reciprocal ties between matrikin

> Now no one has *abusua*. The *abusua* system is completely dead. As I sit here, I am for myself. Finish" (male, age 25–35, Apinaman).
>
> "The *abusua* system is no longer working because our numbers have increased so one cannot afford to keep both nephews and children" (female, age 25–35, Apinaman).
>
> "There is no more *abusua* help. Times are difficult and everyone wants to narrow themselves to their own wife and children" (male, age 35–45, Apinaman).
>
> "There is no *abusua* system nowadays because no one cares for another" (male, age 25–35, Apinaman).
>
> "The *abusua* system collapsed a long time ago and everyone is for their own self" (female, age 25–35, Apinaman).
>
> "The *abusua* system is not working anymore because everyone is giving birth so everyone only helps his or her children" (female, age 21–25, Dwenease).
>
> "The *abusua* system no longer works. Maybe your father is the only one who can help you, but you cannot even rely upon him because the children are many" (male, age 25–35, Dwenease).
>
> "The *abusua* system has collapsed because there is no money. People cannot feed themselves let alone their relatives" (female, age 25–35, Dwenease).
>
> "The *abusua* system no longer works because of hardship and misfortune. Everyone is suffering so how can you help another" (male, age 25–35, Dwenease).
>
> "The *abusua* system only works when you are dead [i.e. at funerals when all kin come around]. But when you are sick no one will care for you. This is because everyone is thinking of their own self" (female age 25–35, Dwenease).

Land shortage and labour service

At the heart of this decline in reciprocating ties of kinship is a crisis in the organisation of farm labour. In the past farm labour within the family was organised on the basis of service. Juniors and wives worked for their seniors and they were eventually rewarded with gifts of farms and inheritance of farm property. Labour service worked in the context of colonisation of a frontier of uncultivated land and an expanding cocoa economy. With expanding economic opportunity the process of frontier colonisation could be intensified with the hiring of migrant labour and sharecropping arrangements with migrant farmers. This process of labour service became complicated with the development of an increasingly commoditised economy, with new perceived needs and the expansion of new economic sectors linking the rural to the urban world. Youth increasingly became dissatisfied with working and being fed by their elders in return for future rewards of land, and expected to be provided with education, apprenticeship, better clothing, access to medical services, and money. They sought alternative economic activities that could provide them with money, and they moved into wage labour, casual labour, and petty trading. They migrated into the district towns, regional capitals and cities.

With the decline of uncultivated land and growing population, the youth became increasingly dependent upon their seniors to provide them with land. They could no longer gain access to land by clearing portions of land in *kwae* areas that had been opened up by their fathers and uncles. This gave greater powers to their seniors to enforce dependent labour services in return for gifts of land:

> Now the youth have no *kwae* on which they can clear their own farm. So it is only their parents who can find them some land. But this depends on how good or serviceable you have been to your father or your mother before they will give you land (male youth at Dwenease).

This perception was echoed in the comments of an elderly man at Apinaman:

> I bought my land for my personal use. Although I can give some to my nephews I may not give them any if I so please. I will share my land according to the service and attendance given me.

Another man at Dwenease in his early forties recounted:

> Not all children are assured land because it is now small. My father decided to give me his land because I stayed with him while the other children continued with their schooling.

An old man in his sixties at Dwenease, said: "I got a bigger share of land because of my service to my father".

With growing reliance on labour service from youth, the position of the sister's son becomes increasingly insecure. The nephew is supposed to receive his training from his father and work with his father on the farm, but at the same time he gains land from his mother's brother. However, population growth results in many nephews vying for the property of a mother's brother, and before the sisters' sons will inherit the junior brothers of the mother's brother have rights to the land. This can lead to many disputes over family land. As one old man at Dwenease commented:

> The *abusua* system is not working anymore. I made a farm on *abusua* land and the farm has now been seized from me by the *abusua*.

Thus, many young men prefer to work with their father rather than their mother's brother, knowing they will secure a gift of a small plot of land or the grant of a portion on which to make a farm.

The granting of land to children has been bolstered by the Interstate Succession Law (PNDC Law 111) of 1985, which gives children rights to inherit the property of their parents and specifies the proportion of property that goes to children. The rights of children and wives are given higher priority than those of the extended family. However, there is difficulty in applying this law to matrilineal property, since several sets of parents have rights to particular plots of land. Nevertheless, this law strengthens the attempts of fathers to pass on their property to their children. This enables people to construct arguments in favour of inheritance by children on the basis of government legislation:

> Now *abusua* is just wife, husband and children. In the past, when one was in trouble the whole family contributed to help you. But not now. This is because the government has changed the inheritance law (female , age 21–25, Dwenease).

The position of fathers is also vulnerable and subject to constraints. While fathers need the labour of their sons and can reward them with gifts of land in return for labour service, they can only give land to their sons and daughters from their personal land, that is agricultural land they have created by clearing uncultivated, mature forest or land they have purchased. The option of clearing forest land has now been curtailed by the disappearance of uncultivated *kwae*. Thus fathers are left with options of purchasing land—which they can farm in their own right with their sons and allocate them portions as gifts—or allocating them portions of land which was allocated by their own fathers as gifts and never came under the control of their father's *abusua*. Fathers may have thrown off responsibilities towards nephews in favour of their sons. But they have less control over land and only access to dwindling supplies of land which they can effectively allocate as gifts to their children. Sons frequently find the areas of land allocated to them by their fathers insufficient and inadequate, and seek to gain land through other circuits. At Apinaman a significant number of men gain access to land through appealing to grandparents. The grandparent generation were often the last to have met large areas of uncultivated forest. They grew up in a period of economic boom marked by expansion of the cocoa economy. They cleared and organised the clearing of large tracts of land for cocoa cultivation, and have significantly larger areas under their care than their parents. Thus at Apinaman, many men gained land through their father's mother rather than their father. Instead of serving a father who cannot help them, some youth rather focus their attentions on their grandparents. One man at Apinaman between 35–45 years of age said:

> My father's mother left the land to me. It's because of the good I did her that she gave me the land. She gave it to me and my brother and we bought one sheep, one piece of cloth and some drink as thank you payment.

Another Apinaman youth, aged between 25–35, gained his land by helping his father's father:

> I used to accompany my father's father to the farm, so when he became old he gave me a plot of land.

An alternative strategy for youth is to go into a sharecropping contract with another farmer. The contract will guarantee the tenant at least a 50 percent share of the crop immediately, without the frustration of a long period of dependency on the father for vague promises of future land. The tenant can also get large areas of land, even if only by making several sharecrop contracts with several farmers. At Dwenease, while the dominant mode of transmission of land from one generation of men to the next is now through the father, more men gain access to land through sharecropping than through their fathers: 34 percent of men in the main survey were farming on sharecropping land and 27 percent gained land from their father. At Apinaman although fewer men sharecropped than at Dwenease, sharecropping was still a dominant mode of gaining access to land. Fathers may also choose to give their land out to sharecrop tenants rather than to give portions to "unreliable" sons who work "halfheartedly" for them.

A significant proportion of youth also give up entirely on agriculture, and seek alternative forms of livelihood. In the past gold mining was the dominant alternative livelihood to agriculture. However, the surface gold deposits have become almost exhausted around this area of the Atewa Range. Those still wishing to mine have moved to Saaman. Others have gone into carrying timber boards for chainsaw operators, from where they have been cut to the roadside. With the decline of gold mining a large number of youth have migrated to towns and cities. Because of problems in getting land other youth remaining in agriculture have decided to illicitly farm within the Atewa Forest Reserve. As one youth recounted:

> I was a driver between Kumasi and Wa. After some time my car owner learned to drive and he took the car away from me. I then decided to return home and farm. But I could not get any land from my relatives so I decided to go into *abunu* sharecropping. The land I got was still insufficient so together with a few friends we decided to enter the forest reserve and make our farms. Then about four years ago the Forestry Guards found our farms and came and slashed down the plantain and other food crops on our farms saying that we had no right to farm in the forest reserve since it was government land. Fortunately, for us, when they left the plantain put out new suckers which yielded well and helped defray part of the debt from our loss of the crops. The following year a lot more youth came to join us in farming within the forest and now we feed from there. It is not that we deliberately like to break the law, but what can we do?

A large percentage of male youth are no longer reliant on land given to them by their kin for farming and have now withdrawn their labour from their fathers and mother's brothers. The senior generation of farmers are forced to hire labour or to lease out their land on a sharecrop basis, when

Box 3.3

The youth do not respect: Youth, land and non-farm activities

"Because of gold mining the youth have money and are not reliant on the elders and do as they please. A lot of them are also travelling out of Apinaman" (male, age 35–45, Apinaman).

"Now the youth do not respect anyone. You send a child to do something for you and they may decide to go or not to go. Many of the youth have left because they don't like farming. When it comes to Christmas the place is full of youth but they all leave after the celebration" (male, age 35–45, Apinaman).

"The youth no longer respect their elders because they can carry boards and go for gold digging. In the old days you could send a child on an errand and if he refused to go you would only tell him 'okay, we will see where you will eat from' and they will get up and run, but now they have got money in their own pocket so they won't mind you at all" (male, age 25–35, Apinaman).

"Gold and diamond mining has given the youth money with which they can buy what they want" (female, age 35–45, Apinaman).

"Because the family cannot take care of them the youth refuse to go to farm with their elders" (male, age 35–45, Apinaman).

"The diamond and gold mining in this town has spoiled the youth" (male, age 25–35, Apinaman).

"Times have changed—everyone is for themselves—so the youth also do what they like" (female, age 35–40, Dwenease).

"The youth do not respect their elders because they are frustrated because their parents cannot afford to help them" (female, age 45–60, Dwenease).

"Because there is no work for them and their parents cannot look after them they have to fend for themselves" (male, age 35–45, Dwenease).

"Because the world is hard now I have no money to give my children so wherever they pass they have to fend for themselves" (female, age 25–35, Dwenease).

they do not have the strength to farm or the money to hire labour. Since migrant farm labour has been in short supply following the Aliens Compliance Order, the elders are in effect forced to pay youth for labour, which was originally provided by their own family youth as a service. At Apinaman, 67 percent of respondents hired labour on their farms, including 62 percent of men and 77 percent of women. In weeding their farm plots, 65 percent of respondents hired labour, including 72 percent of men and 56 percent of women. Similarly at Dwenease, 71 percent of the respondents hired labour on their farm, including 62 percent of men and 77 percent of women. In weeding, 62 percent of respondents hired labour, including 50 percent of men and 70 percent of women. This high dependence on hired labour is reflected at Apinaman by an equally high number of youth who hire out themselves as casual labour. 84 percent of male respondents under the age of 45 hire themselves out as casual daily-labour. This includes 80 percent of those between 26–35 years of age, 89 percent of those between

36–45 years of age and 50 percent of those in the 46–60 age group. However, this trend is not as pronounced at Dwenease where only 43 percent of men engage in hiring themselves out as casual farm labour. This includes only 27 percent of the under 45 age group, 17 percent of those in the 26–35 age group, 50 percent in the 36–45 age group and 38 percent of those in the 46–60 age group. This reflects a breakdown in family labour and the commodification of labour within smallholder farm production. This breakdown of farm labour leads to perceptions of inter-generational conflict and a lack of respect among the youth for their elders (see Box 3.3).

Land sales

Selling land is an alternative to farming in one's own right with children or to sharecropping. The sale of land is usually justified in terms of hardship and pressure to meet the needs of dependants for medical bills, school fees, to renovate family houses, and to finance funerals. These are considered legitimate reasons for selling matrilineal land, since the lineage is bound to meet the social welfare requirements of its members. Beyond these distress reasons for selling land, land sales often result from problems with matrilineal land. This may occur as a result of disputes over who has rights to cultivate the land, or problems in sharing the land between all the heirs, or because the land is in an unfavourable location, or from the frustrations of not being able to afford to hire sufficient labour, and declining profitability of farming. In some cases there are tacit agreements to break up matrilineal property for artificial expenditures. One man claimed that he had sold land to meet the costs of educating a son. Further investigations revealed that he was using the proceeds to erect his own individual house. Other arrangements can be worked out in which a family dependant claims to be sick and land is sold to meet spurious medical bills. The breaking up of matrilineal lands enables the hold of family members on property transmission to be undermined. Household heads can sell matrilineal land and then use parts of the proceeds to purchase their own land, which will be free from demands and pulls of matrilineal members. As one man in his forties dryly commented:

> The *abusua* can only help by selling the family properties if there is a problem. Otherwise each and everyone for themselves.

A young Apinaman man in his early twenties further remarked:

> If you come from a good family they still cater for you. But almost everyone is now independent and people are selling their family land.

In the main survey 94 percent of the respondents at Apinaman and 83 percent at Dwenease felt that there was a ready land market in operation, that if you wanted to buy land it was easy to find willing vendors. However, more

Box 3.4 *Land sales in the Atewa Range settlements*

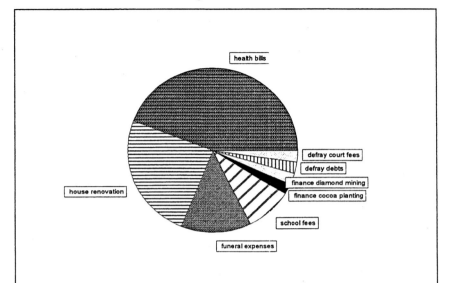

A survey of land sales in both Apinaman and Dwenease revealed 36 cases of which 15 were recorded for Apinaman and 21 for Dwenease. Sixteen cases of land sales were transacted by women and 20 by men. The main reasons for selling land were to raise medical fees for a family member (56% of cases), for renovation of house (31%), for raising money to meet funeral costs (17%) and for children's school fees (11%). Other reasons were to raise money for planting cocoa (3%), to raise money for gaining access to rights to win diamonds in a concession (3%), to defray debts (3%) and to get rid of unfavourably situated on hilly ground (3%). The majority of land was sold to people from neighbouring settlements. Sixty percent of respondents claimed that the purchasers of the land came from neighbouring settlements, 21 percent were strangers from outside the area and 19 percent of land sales were to local people.

people were aware of actual cases of land sales within their families at Dwenease than at Apinaman. 31 percent of respondents at Dwenease knew of cases where members of their family had sold land as compared to 20 percent at Apinaman. This would seem to reflect the greater land shortage at Dwenease. This creates a high demand for a land market, where anyone with a financial problem can find a ready buyer for land. An alliance may develop between vari‹ break up matrilineal la which becomes free of at Dwenease could als‹ ing land from their fath

At Apinaman, lanc shortage and demand levels of capital forma people from buying land. In this situation there are more people willing to

sell than to purchase land. This could favour the alienation of family property to large-scale capitalist farmers from outside the settlement. This is
already beginning to happen on Apinaman land, where some large-scale
farmers from outside the area have purchased land to develop commercial
ventures. One commercial farmer has established a large coffee plantation.

The matrifocal alliance and the significance of male spouses

The Interstate Succession Law is often justified in terms of supporting the
rights of women and children. However, this only supports the rights of
women as wives. The Interstate Succession Law does not cater for situations
in which there is instability of marriage, large incidence of divorces and
serial marriages, large numbers of children born outside of marriage, and
widespread male poverty leading to inability to maintain wives and children.

At Apinaman and Dwenease a significant proportion of women do not
look to security through rights in the property of their husbands, but
through establishing their own rights in land and rights to control land.
They seek to pass on their own farm property to their daughters. The basis
of this alliance is the gender division of labour within the household in
which sons work with their fathers and daughters with their mothers and
grandmothers. Inter-generational conflicts between mothers and daughters
over the organisation of farm labour are not marked by the intensity of
conflicts between men. This is partly because women's farming is not as
commodity oriented as men. Daughters are often content to farm alongside
their mothers on the mother's farm until they are married, since they lack
the capital and strength to manage farm labour. Women farm smaller areas
and focus more on food crops than orchard crops.

The basis of the matrifocal alliance is essentially to ensure that female
descendants gain access to land, and to prevent male descendants monopo-
lising land and passing it on to their sons. At Apinaman, one woman la-
mented: "My brother has taken over all the land and does not want to give
us some". Given land shortage and the various strategies being used by
male youth to circumvent the labour demands of mother's brothers and
fathers, many sons may attempt to acquire land from their mothers. Access
to land for the next generation of women largely depends upon that transmitted by their mothers. Their interests in land are dependent upon their
mothers giving them priority in the transmission of land and in retaining
female property as female property. Daughters help their mothers with the
knowledge that their mothers will ensure their future rights to land, and
prevent their land being alienated to their brothers. Thus mothers may
allow their sons rights to cultivate land temporarily, but less frequently
alienate land to them as gifts:

Women usually pass on their land to their daughters and granddaughters but give land to their sons to work on temporarily (young women in twenties, Dwenease).

Women's land usually goes to the daughters. At times they give the boys land to feed on but do not give it out as a gift to their boys (male, late fifties, Dwenease).

Mothers' mothers play an important role in this strategy in the present era. They were able to acquire significant tracts of land during the early cocoa boom, which are often larger than the individual tracts that their sons have at their disposal. The daughter helps the mother in establishing her farms. The mother gives the daughter land to work on independently. As her daughters mature, they also help their mother on her own independent farms and those she works with the grandmother. The grandmother frequently leaves land to the granddaughters. Since the serious task of women farming independently occurs when women have finished with childbearing, when their oldest children have reached their twenties, it is the grandmothers who have established farm property to give to their granddaughters.

Matrifocal interests in land are often articulated in terms of protecting matrilineal rights in lands. This argument notes the contradiction in the role of males as providers for sons and wives with matrilineal ethics. It portrays sons as matrilineal imposters, who will alienate matrilineal lands to their wives and sons and thus threaten the future survival of matrilineal property. As one young woman at Apinaman elaborated:

> We are three sisters and a brother. Our mother's brother is dead and has left a large tract of land for us, which is lying fallow. We are planning to meet here to share the land among us. We are planning that we will not give our brother any part of the land because if we allow him to develop part he will eventually leave it to his children. So he has to find his own land elsewhere, since he is not going to marry from our family. We can develop what is there little by little for our children.

Box 3.5 provides a spectrum of views on reasons why women transmit property to their daughters. These stress that men break up family property and parcel it out to their sons and wives as gifts. Their sons and wives belong to other matrilineages. In contrast women's children belong to the matrilineage. However, their male children will eventually marry outside of the matrilineage and their children will belong to another matrilineage. Thus, it is argued that given the propensity of men to look after their own children in the present period rather than their sisters' children, the genuine custodians of matriliny are the female children of women. A second discourse on women, land and matriliny concerns the role of husbands. This focuses on the fact that the children of women married to outside spouses

Box 3.5

Women ass land to their daughters because men don't belong

"Women usually pass on their land to their daughters and granddaughters. That is the tradition here because men don't belong to the abusua" (male youth, age 25–35, Apinaman).

"Women pass on most of their land to their daughters. This becomes abusua land" (male, age 25–35, Apinaman).

"Here all family land usually comes from the mother's side. A father can always give out his land as a gift to his children. In that case it becomes their own property which they can sell out and develop for their own use" (woman, age 25–35, Dwenease).

"Women usually pass on their land to their daughters and granddaughters because if they give it to the male children the plot goes to another family" (male, age 35–45, Dwenease).

"Women usually pass on their land to their daughters and granddaughters because if you give it to the son it goes out of the family but for the women it will stay in the home" (woman, age 21–25, Dwenease).

"Women usually pass on their land to their daughters and granddaughters so that the land remains in the family" (woman, age 21–25, Dwenease).

"If they give the land to the boys it will go to another family so they usually give to the girls" (male, age 25–35, Dwenease).

"Women usually pass on their land to their daughters and granddaughters because if they give it to the male children they take it out of the house" (male, age 44, Dwenease).

"Women usually pass on their land to their daughters and granddaughters so that the land will stay back in the same house" (woman, age 35–45, Dwenease).

"Women usually pass on their land to their daughters and granddaughters because if you give it to the boys it will go out of the abusua" (woman, age 21–25, Dwenease).

"Women usually pass on their land to their daughters and granddaughters because if you give it to the boys, and they happen to give birth, the land goes to the boy's wife's children" (woman, under 21, Dwenease).

belong to the matrilineage, while the children of wives of male members of the *abusua* belong to other lineages. If a husband helps a wife on her farm and the land goes to their children, the land has been transferred to members of the matrilineage. Thus when women marry, their mothers give them portions of land for their husband to work on for them and create wealth for them and their children:

> When I got married I decided to see my mother to give me a portion of land to farm. So she gave me part of her portion of land on which I am working (woman, age 25–35, Apinaman).

> I used to help my mother on the farm and when I got married I told her to give me a place to make my own farm and she gave me part of her land (woman, age 25–35, Apinaman).

> When I got married to my wife her mother have us the plot to farm and eat from (male, age 25–35, Apinaman).

> Women give their land to their daughters. Usually the daughter's husband works on the land (male, age 44, Apinaman).

The matrifocal discourse can stress that husbands are more reliable farmers than are brothers, since they are being watched by wives who the land belongs to, who will choose responsible men as husbands, and divorce them if they do not meet expectations:

> The land is for all of us children (male and female) except that the men may be lazy while we women depend upon our husbands for farming activities (woman, age 25–35, Apinaman).

For this strategy to be successful, the men must not have access to sufficient land in their own right to establish their own autonomous farms and get their wives to labour for them:

> Women usually prefer to give land to their daughters because the daughters are looked after by men. These men need some land to be able to work on and they help the women on their farms (male, age 25, Dwenease).

> Three plots of my land are from my wife. She got them from her mother. It will go to my children. I have also bought one plot of land (male, age 35–45, Apinaman).

This strategy is most successful when the husband is a migrant, without land in the area:

> I am a carpenter by profession from the Volta Region. I took my wife from this town and her parents gave me this plot of land to develop, which I have started doing this year (male migrant, age 25–35, Apinaman).

> I came from the Volta Region and married here. When I got married my mother-in-law decided to give the land we are farming on to my wife as a gift. We in turn gave one goat, one bottle of imported Schnapps and cedi (¢) 15,000 as thanks (*aseda*) to her (male migrant, age 25–35, Apinaman).

As land becomes increasingly scarce, marriage may form an important avenue through which young men gain access to land (but with new responsibilities). In the most developed form of matrifocal interest there is an implicit call that women as wives and mothers should replace men as uncles or brothers as the main transmitters of land:

> Women usually pass on their land to their daughters and granddaughters because if the men marry they will have to get some land for their wives. So women also marry and have their husbands work on their land for them (woman, age 33, Dwenease).

Women usually pass on their land to their daughters and granddaughters because the man can always get some land from the in-laws when they marry,
but the land at home [in the family] remains there when given to daughters
(woman, age 21–25, Dwenease).

The advantages in women transmitting property on which their husbands
work is that there is no conflict between children and the matrilineage, and
no individual alienation of land away from matrilineal interests. The matrifocal strategy can also be seen as overcoming the pressures of inter-generational conflicts over control of land and labour, and the commodification of
land and labour. Rather than hiring labour, women rely on their husbands
to labour or hire labour, and children work alongside their mothers knowing they will definitely inherit the land without any conflicts between the
rights of different matrilineal members and the rights of fathers to give
matrilineal land as gifts to children. And where women do not have husbands they can still gain access to land through their mothers and grandmothers.

A latent contradiction exists in the matrifocal-spouse alliance. If the interests of the man are gained on the basis that his children will inherit the
land, this in effect means that male children will also inherit portions, which
they may want to transmit to their own wives and children from other
matrilineages. This could erode the consolidation of land under the matrifocal alliance and lead to men alienating women's property. The ambivalence
of this position is reflected in perceptions of the inheritance of women's
land. While the transmission of land from mother to daughter is statistically
dominant, a significant proportion of respondents felt that women gave
their land to both male and female children (see Table 3.2).

Table 3.2 *The transmission of women's property to daughters and sons*

Transmission of women's Property (*percentage*)	Apinaman			Dwenease		
	Male	Female	Total	Male	Female	Total
Goes to daughters only	50	54	52	76	68	73
Goes to sons and daughters	35	46	40	17	26	21
Don't know	15	.	8	7	5	6
No. of respondent	26	24	50	29	19	48

Land at Kofi Pare

In contrast with the two Atewa Range settlements, Kofi Pare is a settlement
of migrants. The heart of this settlement is the land purchased by migrant
settlers from Aburi. While these migrants are matrilineal, as the Atewa
Range settlements, since the 1960s other migrant sections purchasing land
adjacent to Kofi Pare have moved from the small villages and isolated
homesteads they established on their farms into Kofi Pare town. Many of

these migrants are from groups who practise patrilineal descent. These groups have impacted on the social and economic structure of Kofi Pare. They play a major role in sharecropping on land owned by Aburi farmers, which has an important effect on the transfer of land from one generation to the next.

Kofi Pare town is named after Kofi Pare, the Aburi man who bought the most substantial portion of Kofi Pare land from Akyem chiefs at Akateng. The descendants of Kofi Pare trace their origins back to Sakyikrom and Nsakyi and to Akwamu, from where it is claimed that Kofi Pare's maternal grandfather originated. From there, Kofi Pare's father, Nana Danso, his junior brother, Mensah Akoanankrom and Kofi Pare purchased land at Pakro (Parekrom, that is Pare town). The profits which Kofi Pare gained from farming at Pakro were used to purchase land at Kofi Pare.

Hill (1963) records that Kofi Pare had six associates with whom he purchased the land. These associates were all related, although they were not all matrilineal relatives. Four of the groups came from Kofi Pare's maternal side and three from other matrilineages. The land was divided among these seven associates according to their contribution. These seven associates subsequently divided their share among their relatives, giving portions to both matrilineal and patrilineal relatives. These seven sections remain distinct to this day. The lands within these sections have not been subdivided into small plots of land with defined boundaries which are then further subdivided among the next generation of heirs. The descendants have gained rights to the use of land, rather than to particular plots of land. Cocoa farms are inherited rather than the land. Thus the land inherited by subsequent generations follows the extension and contraction of plantations. Hill (1963) records that in 1959 there were 137 farmers registered as owning land within the surveyed area and 49 farmers within Kofi Pare's section. Today there are about 45 farmers with claims to ownership of farms within the Kofi Pare section, of whom five are women. The land has been inherited by both children and maternal relatives of Kofi Pare.

When Kofi Pare first came to the land, he was followed by his brother Kwadjo Danso and his maternal nephews Yaw Kwafo and Yaw Akotuah. The nephews helped Kofi Pare on his farms and Kofi Pare gave them land on which to make their own cocoa farms. They would take time off working on Kofi Pare's land to establish their own farms. These farms were inherited by their nephews and children who in turn had helped them to establish their own farms. Both children (in the paternal line) and matrilineal relatives have inherited land at Kofi Pare.

Kofi Pare did not only rely on his relatives to establish his cocoa farms. He also had many labourers working for him, including Fantis, Wangaras, Chambas, Zambarama, and some Akuapem. Some of these were rewarded for service with plots of land. For instance, Kwame Owu came to work as a labourer for Kofi Pare. He worked hard, but could not save enough money to purchase his own land, so Kofi Pare eventually rewarded him with a plot of land. Many other landowners at Kofi Pare have also relied on caretakers to manage their farm and have been absentee farmers. Thus, in the heyday of cocoa migrant labourers made up a significant part of Kofi Pare's population. Through his labourers, Kofi Pare was able to extend his own cocoa plantations and maintain existing farms.

Table 3.3 *Division of Land at Kofi Pare in the 1950s*

	Number of sub-groups							
	1	2	3	4	5	6	7	Total
Head of sub-group or his successor:								
Acreage	84.0	138.2	75.9	34.8	62.1	50.7	20	465.7
No. of farmers	(1)	(1)	(1)	(1)	(1)	(1)	(1)	(7)
Average acreage	84.0	138.2	75.9	34.8	62.1	50.7	20	66.5
Maternal relatives of head of sub-group:								
Acreage	139.8	18.3	85.9	48.9	35.1	13.1	20.9	362.0
No. of farmers	(18)	(9)	(11)	(4)	(3)	(6)	(4)	(55)
Average acreage	7.8	2.0	7.8	12.2	11.7	2.2	5.2	6.6
Sons and daughters of head of sub-group or his successor:								
Acreage	66.9	.	19	3.9	6.1	.	1	96.9
No. of farmers	(7)	.	(7)	(1)	(3)	.	(1)	(19)
Average acreage	9.6		2.7	3.9	2.0		1.0	5.1
Other:								
Acreage	81.5	12.6	20.6	.	23.1	89.7	.	227.5
No. of farmers	(23)	(1)	(11)	.	(12)	(14)	.	(61)
Average acreage	3.5	12.6	1.9		1.9	6.4		3.7

Source: Hill (1963)

While the seven associates who purchased the land distributed plots to relatives and others who had served them, the majority of the recipients of land received small portions, and the original associates retained the lions' share of the land. Hill (1963) records that apart from the seven heads of the sub-groups, only 6 other farmers had farms of more than 20 acres. While the average size of land farmed by the original associates or their successors was 66.5 acres, those farmed by matrilineal relatives was 6.6 acres, those by children was 5.1 acres and those by the other category was 3.7 acres. The "other" category was the largest category constituting 43 percent of the population of the settlement. These figures suggest that the basis of parcelling out land to relatives is not a horizontal solidarity based on concepts of equity, but a vertical solidarity based on service. Hill (1963) argues that the development of migrant cocoa farming reflected a "classlessness" which promoted a "universal participation: "there are rich people and poor people, but none who suffer from a social inferiority preventing them from migrating" (1963:182). However, she acknowledges that this participation was often based on pre-existing social relations reflecting ties of dependency and notions of service:

> The fact that in the early days the richer inhabitants were often prepared to help their poorer kinsmen and neighbours to buy land through companies, by lending them money, sometimes on the security of pawns, is another aspect of the willingness to wait for a return on money—though it is even truer then than it is today that the condition of indebtedness was apt to reflect a pre-existing relationship between the two parties, their being no concept of large-scale philanthropy in the Akwapim towns (1963:182).

The early migrant cocoa farmers, needed to recruit followers to help them create viable rural settlements, undertake infrastructure building, and provide them with labour services, including farm labour and carriers/porters,[12] in lieu of the absence of a labour market. It was only after the creation of a rural infrastructure that migrant labour would begin to move into these areas in search of work. Hill (1963) notes that employment of labourers was associated with the second stage of cocoa expansion, rather than the first. It is when farmers have successfully established bearing cocoa plantations, that they use part of the proceeds to employ labour:

> But although nearly all Akwapim farmers who own large farms, of (say) twenty acres or more, employ labourers (sometimes a great many of them) and although many quite small farmers do likewise (an element of prestige being involved), it is important to note that systematic employment of farm labourers marked the second, not the first stage of the developing capitalist process ...
>
> The second stage in the developing capitalist process was reached when the farmer had successfully established a sufficient area of bearing cocoa *to support a labourer from its proceeds*. On his first employment the labourer might be entitled to 'use' all the cocoa he plucked from the young farm on condition that he assisted the farmer in establishing new cocoa-farms, which later on, he would have the right to harvest. As the yield of this original farm increased, the proportion of the crop to which he was entitled fell to one-third—the traditional *abusa* share. Later on, perhaps seven to ten years after his first employment, he might (especially if he had not been concerned with the original

---

[12] These were used to carry cocoa and food stuffs to market for sale and also for carrying items to the settlement.

establishment of the farm in question) be transferred to the *nkotokuano*[13] basis, receiving a certain sum always less than one third of the value of the cocoa. The labourer who harvested the cocoa was always paid, on a piece-work basis, *from the proceeds of the farm at the time of the sale of the produce*—the farmer thus avoiding the use of working capital. Although a farmer who employed labourers was free, as a consequence, to devote more time to 'management' and could more quickly develop newly acquired lands farther west, he would not himself stop working on the land, though certain tasks, such as plucking and weeding, tended to devolve more and more on labourers as time went on (1963:189).

The process of establishing frontier cocoa farms began with the farmer attracting labour from his personal network of relatives and dependants. Larger numbers of dependants enabled cocoa farmers to establish plantations rapidly and move from the first stage to the second, when they could employ hired labour and begin to develop new land. Thus by giving out a large number of small parcels to relatives, the large matrilineal migrant farmers would be assured a large supply of non-monetary labour which could be used to develop their farm and infrastructure. Hill (1963:189) estimates that the transition from the first to the second stage could take place after between five years to twenty-five years depending on the relatives and dependants the farmers could attract to help them.

The plots of land given to the majority of matrilineal relations were small. This in effect reinforced ties of dependency. Since the plot cannot cater for the needs of all the descendants of the dependent relatives, these relatives will in turn become dependent upon those with land, and will need to establish new relations of service in return for access to land or some form of contractual relationship based on exchange of land for labour or a portion of the product of labour. This results in a large number of present day farmers suffering from land shortage. At Kofi Pare 64 percent of respondents felt they had insufficient land to meet their farming requirements, including 74 percent of males and 50 percent of females.

This leads to a social structure which is distinct from that associated with the Atewa Range settlements. While in the Atewa Range settlements, the elements of service in the past were associated with relations between fathers and sons and uncles and nephews, these relations permeate the whole structure of the Aburi migrant matrilineage, in which the land purchaser becomes the father and uncle of the matrilineage, and those granted land the sons and nephews. Thus disparities in land holdings are not only structured inter-generationally, between youth and elders, but also between

---

[13] *Nkotokuano* is a piece rate system in which the labourer receives a fixed sum of money for every cocoa bag harvested from the farm.

the heirs of the original land purchasers who farmed the majority of the land, their matrilineal "followers", and other farmers who came to the land.

A second significant difference lies in the access of women to land. While women could easily gain land in the Atewa Range settlements through fathers and mothers allocating them portions of family land and husbands clearing the land for them, among the migrant farmers, women largely operate as wives of farmers, establishing food crop farms which eventually become cocoa farms owned by their husbands. Unfortunately, Hill does not provide figures on the number of women farming on Kofi Pare land, although we know that only one woman had a farm of over 20 acres. During the recent survey, in the section of land which originally belonged to Kofi Pare, 49 farmers were now farming there, of whom only five were women.

Hill (1963) noted that, in general, Akuapem women were rarely part of the original land owning associates that purchased land for cocoa farming. Women usually went to the cocoa frontier as wives of husbands and were engaged in cultivating food crops on their husband's land. Hill contrasts the situation of the migrant cocoa farmers, who were largely male, with the native Akyem farmers with smaller farms, in which "nearly half" of the farms were owned by women. The organisation of migrant cocoa farmers was essentially based on the alliances of men, joint investment and coopera- tion between brothers, fathers, sons and matrilineal kin, and between sisters' husbands and sisters' brothers. The second type of relationship was one of dependence between poorer matrilineal kin and other dependants providing labour service to richer patrons who provided them with land.

These characteristics are reflected in the difference in landholding in Kofi Pare and the Atewa Range settlements. This pattern for Kofi Pare is shown in Table 3.4. In contrast with the Atewa settlements, the matrifocal alliance is largely absent. Although some women do gain land from their mothers, a larger percent gain land from their fathers. Land is largely controlled and transmitted by men. As in the Atewa Range settlements fathers have usurped the role of mother's brothers in the transmittance of land. At Apinaman 15 percent of male respondents and 10 percent of the sample gained land from their mother's brother. At Dwenease 10 percent of male respondents and 7 percent of the sample acquired land from their mother's brother. In the Aburi section (that is the matrilineal section)[14] of Kofi Pare 18 percent of male respondents and 9 percent of the sample gained land from their mother's brother. Only 2 percent of male respondent at Apinaman and 29 percent of males at Dwenease gained land from their father. But in the

---

[14] Since the other sections of Kofi Pare are dominated by people who inherit land patrilineally it is pointless comparing them with the Atewa sections for features of matrilineal kin.

Aburi section of Kofi Pare 47 percent of male respondents gained land from their fathers. Among women respondents 45 percent of those at Kofi Pare gained land from their father as compared to 4 percent at Apinaman and 32 percent at Dwenease. While 59 percent of women at Apinaman and 43 percent at Dwenease gained land from their mother or mother's mother, only 28 percent of female respondents gained land from their mother or mother's mother. The maternal grandmother was absent as a bestower of land at Kofi Pare. The other characteristic of the matrifocal alliance is also absent at Kofi Pare. Male spouses do not farm on their wife's land. It is common for women to be dependent upon their husband for land rather than provide land for their husband to work on. Thus the control and transmittance of land is firmly under the control of men and fathers.

Table 3.4 *Source of land at Kofi Pare*

Source of land	Aburi section			Non-Aburi section			Kofi Pare settlement		
	Male	Female	Total	Male	Female	Total	Male	Female	Total
Purchase	.	.	.	11	.	8	6	.	3
Sharecrop	41	22	32	61	13	50	52	23	39
Hiring	.	.	.	6	13	8	3	4	3
Father	47	45	46	22	13	19	34	35	33
Mother	6	28	17	.	25	8	3	27	13
Wofa	18	.	9	.	.	.	9	4	5
Spouse	.	11	6	.	13	4	.	11	5
Mother's mother	.	.	.	.	13	4	.	4	2
Father's father	.	.	.	6	.	4	3	.	2
None	.	6	3	.	.	.	.	4	2
No. of respondents	17	18	35	18	8	26	35	26	61

Another important characteristic of the Kofi Pare land is the dominance of sharecropping. In contrast to the Atewa settlements, sharecropping is not only confined to men, but nearly a quarter of Aburi women gain access to land by sharecropping. Nearly 40 percent of respondents sharecropped. This figure is higher for the non-Aburi farmers than the Aburi farmers. Fifty percent of non-Aburi farmers sharecropped as compared to 32 percent of Aburi farmers, and 61 percent of non-Aburi male farmers sharecropped as compared to 41 percent of Aburi males. Thus sharecropping is the most important mode of non-Aburi farmers gaining access to land, and is almost on a par with land allocated by fathers among the Aburi farmers. A large proportion of men are not dependent upon the labour of their sons and nephews on their farms but prefer to give their land to sharecrop tenants. Conversely, a large number of youth are forced to engage in sharecropping arrangements to gain access to farm land because of land shortage within their families, or prefer a sharecropping contract rather than working with their father or uncle on the understanding of gaining land in future.

The family system

Similar perceptions exist to those in the Atewa Range settlements, of a family system in decline rooted in growing hardship and the increasing size of families without sufficient resources to cater for the needs of their members:

> The family system has declined because our population has increased and the land is small so everyone has to find their own way (woman, age 49, Aburi).

> The family system has declined because the world is now so difficult that everyone has to care for their children and no one else. But in the old days life was cheap. In the cocoa farm there was every type of food and the people were few (woman, age 45–60, Dodowa).

The role of the mother's brothers is perceived to have declined because they cannot cater for the growing needs of their sisters' children:

> If you are in a family with money everyone runs to you and says *wofa* [mother's brother], if in trouble. But if you don't have money no one comes to you or cares for you (male, age 42, Aburi).

The authority of elders over youth has declined as a result of an inability to provide them with their basic needs, security, access to land and livelihood support. Youth are increasingly autonomous, gaining their livelihoods outside of the agricultural sector or moving into wage labour and petty trading in the urban areas:

> Because their parents cannot care for them the youth have to find their own money and so do not respect the elders (woman, age 35–45, Accra).

> If you don't feed your child how do you expect them to do something for you without any problem occurring? (male, age 25–35, Larteh).

> Youth know where to find their own money so they do not respect their parents any more. They do by-day, carrying of boards and mason work. They leave to Accra and Kumasi where the girls work as chop bar attendants, seamstresses and hairdressers and the boys do carpentry and electrician work (male, under 21, Aburi).

At Kofi Pare, 61 percent of youth under the age of 45 years hired themselves out as casual daily labour (as compared to 8 percent of men over the age of 45 years). This included 100 percent of respondents in the under 25 age category, 78 percent of those in the 26–35 age group and 36 percent in the 36–45 age group. A large percentage of farmers depend upon hired labour: 67 percent of respondents hired labour including 70 percent of men and 65 percent of women. 67 percent of the men hired labour for weeding as did 61 percent of women farmers.

With increasing difficulty of exercising authority over youth within the family for farm services, most men begin to focus on their own children, working with them and passing on their cocoa plantations to them:

> Men usually pass on land to their sons because most men work with their children rather than their nephews (male, age 25–35, Aburi).

In contrast to the Atewa Range, there is no countervailing matrifocal ideology, which challenges the authority of men to give matrilineal land to their sons. In place of this a large number of Aburi women expressed a preference for allocating their land to their male children:

> I give my land to my sons, because if you give to the women it goes to her husband. Although if a girl is named after me I can give a small plot to my daughter in the name of my grandchild (woman, over 60, Aburi).
>
> Women give land to the male children because it is rather the men who will farm" (woman, age 35–45, Aburi).

The main factors militating against the emergence of a matrifocal ideology are rooted in the nature of settlement among migrant Akuapem cocoa farmers. The land is purchased by a group of male associates. Women follow these men to the frontier usually as wives, and sometimes as sisters. The frontier is not conceived as a permanent home and there is mobility between several frontier settlements and the home town. In many instances women born and reared in one of these migrant settlements are likely to move back to their home town at some stage or contract a marriage which takes them out of the migrant settlement. Thus, the women will often "leave the land and go into marriage" elsewhere, resulting in the perception that it is the male children who farm the land or are the stable farmers.

Women play an important role in placing males in that the males trace their relations in terms of their mothers and sisters. But this can also work against the role of women in production. Polly Hill (1963) shows that the relationships of descent and the inheritance of land in the migrant Aburi matrilineal lands were often complicated by marriages. A large number of original land purchasing associates included categories of sisters' brothers and sisters' husbands. This ensured that farm property could be consolidated into the hands of kin who were sons to one category and sisters' sons to another category. A large number of marriages consisted of cross-cousins between categories such as daughters and sisters' sons. While this consolidated the lineage and inheritance ties of the male successors of the original associates, it meant that women's patterns of residence were being determined by male marriage alliances. This would weaken the autonomous ties of kinship between grandmothers, daughters, and granddaughters. In the context of migrant frontier cocoa farming, women lacked the ability to clear or get cleared land they could claim as their own land, and were dependent upon access to land which had been purchased by groups of men for specific investment in cocoa plantations. When women were allocated significant portions of land, it was often with concerns that their male children should inherit that land, and served to provide their sons with access to land to enable them to participate in cocoa farming.

Sharecropping

Within the kinship system more land is being allocated to sons than to nephews. However, in many respects the ascendant land relationship is sharecropping. Among the Aburi section roughly equal numbers of men are dependent upon sharecropping as on descent in gaining access to land. Among the non-Aburi migrants to Kofi Pare more men are dependent upon sharecropping for access to farm land than on land allocated by their senior kinsmen.

Sharecropping is the ultimate weapon of elders who can no longer control their youth and the labour of their family youth on their farms. Faced with youth who are unwilling to work consistently on the farm or to run errands, the elders can allocate land on a share contract to outsiders. The usual terms on established cocoa farms are a division into third shares between the landowner and the tenant with the tenant taking one third. On land in which the tenant establishes the plantation the division between landlord and tenant is equal (half) shares.

Through sharecropping, relations based on reciprocal services are broken in favour of a contractual relationship with an outsider. This enables the elder to gain greater security over the processes of farm labour, since the tenants become responsible for managing and hiring labour, and their farm proceeds depend upon the management of this labour. It also enables elders to get rid of family youth who are not working efficiently in favour of sharecropping tenants. An elder who is not satisfied with the farm service of his youth can tell the youth he is unhappy about the way he is working on the farm and that the proceeds he is receiving from the farm are unsatisfactory. If he feels there is no subsequent improvement he can then allocate the land to a sharecrop tenant. Once this process has occurred the youth from the household of the elder will also be forced to seek land on a sharecrop basis or move out of farm production into an alternative form of livelihood.

Sharecropping may also be a more satisfactory arrangement for youth. They may choose to seek a sharecropping contract rather than serve their elders for a long period before receiving land. This particularly affects nephews who cannot be sure when they will receive land from their uncles, since the land can go through innumerable circuits of brothers before coming down to the next generation. The preferences of an elder to pass on land to a particular nephew may be overridden by other prominent family members and inter-family political disputes over the control of land. Given this situation, a nephew may prefer to seek a sharecropping contract rather than work with his mother's brother.

With the increasing commodification of life, youth need money and elders are not able to provide them with their monetary requirements. Rather than work for their elders, youth may prefer to engage in casual labour and other alternative income-generating activities. This forces elders either to hire labour on their farms or give out land to sharecrop tenants. Elders with insufficient capital to hire labour are forced to give out their land on a sharecropping basis. Thus, sharecropping is not limited to those with large areas of surplus land but also affects smallholders with insufficient capital to hire labour to work their land. In several respects, poorer families may be under more pressure to sharecrop their lands than the richer families. Richer families with large lands can give out lands to their children and nephews, retaining their labour within the family lands, and supplementing their labour with hired labour and sharecrop tenants. In contrast, poorer families have no land to provide for the youth. The youth are forced to work outside the family land as casual labour or sharecrop tenants. In the process their labour is withdrawn from the family labour pool. The elders working the land are forced to hire labour to supplement their own efforts, and when they can no longer afford to hire labour they are forced to sharecrop their land with youth.

Sharecropping increasingly becomes a relationship between elders and youth, reflecting the breakdown of relations based on service. Ultimately, as sharecropping becomes more competitive and youth find it difficult to get access to good land on a sharecrop basis, a reciprocal service relationship between a father and son may be replaced by sharecropping between the two. As one Aburi male youth stated: "The land is for my father but I am only working on it on *abunu* basis".

Land sales

Land sales are not perceived as being as significant at Kofi Pare as in the Atewa Range settlements. Only 19 percent of respondents at Kofi Pare considered it easy to be able to purchase land—as compared with over 80 percent in the Atewa Range This includes 20 percent of Aburi residents and 19 percent of non-Aburi residents.[15] A common sentiment expressed at Kofi Pare is that "Kofi Pare bought all the land here so no one can sell any piece of land in this town". Since all the heirs to Kofi Pare land gained access to the land through their ties to Kofi Pare and hold the land as family land it is not easy for them to sell the land. However, in reality, people do sell land in times of hardship and need. 20 percent of Kofi Pare respondents were able to confirm that they had known a relative to sell land. This included 23 percent of the non-Aburi and 20 percent of the Aburi sections—a figure higher than that recorded for Apinaman. One woman respondent from the non-Aburi section suggested: "If only you are lucky you may get land to buy. Someone may have land but they don't get anything from it—so they decide to sell it". Land can be bought and sold at Kofi Pare, but eager vendors are not as commonplace as at Apinaman.

In contrast to the Atewa Range settlements, Kofi Pare has a more thriving agricultural sector. Its economy is still largely dominated by cocoa, which has been kept alive with support from the Cocoa Rehabilitation Project, with the disbursement of loans and credits to farmers for rehabilitation of plantations, acquisition of seedlings and hiring of labour. Farmers prefer to maintain land and invest in farming rather than sell off the land. Sharecropping provides an alternative way of generating capital from the land rather than land sales. Thus, land sales arise out of desperate needs, misfortunes and debts, such as the need to gain legal representation because of a court case of a family member, sickness, or to offset the debts of a funeral.

Conclusion

In both the Atewa Range settlements and Kofi Pare land ownership is associated with a matrilineal identity. However, this matrilineal identity embodies distinct historical processes that reflect different processes of agricultural capital accumulation. Kofi Pare is the product of the investments of rich Aburi men in land in the nineteenth century. Profits emanating from investments in oil palm in the early nineteenth century were reinvested in the purchase of land in the New Suhum area for cocoa farming. A small number of associates who were usually related through bilateral kinship or marriage often came together to purchase the land and then developed the land into cocoa plantations. The development of the land was dependent upon rallying round supporters who could create a village infrastructure of dwelling places, roads, paths, and provide labour. Settlers were recruited from the

---

[15] The non-Aburi residents bought their lands separate from Kofi Pare. Some of them also bought a portion of the Kofi Pare land that was resold (Hill, 1963). They later came to reside in Kofi Pare Town.

matrilineal segments to which the associates belonged and they were given free parcels of land in return for providing services and help in farm labour to the associates. Once the settlement was opened up, labourers would then begin to congregate in search of work. Since the recruitment of matrilineal relatives was largely for labour in cocoa production, the majority of land was granted to men. While land was given to sisters, this was often with a view to pass it on to their male heirs, and to cement marriage relations among "business" associates and to build up networks of cross-cousins, which would maintain the bulk of property within a small circle of relatives. Landholdings at Kofi Pare were differentiated. A few farmers owned large plots and a large number of small farmers owned small plots. The small farmers performed services for the large farmers who were their senior kinfolk. The smallholders had insufficient land to provide for the needs of their descendants. The descendants negotiated with the large landholders for land on sharecropping arrangements and *abusa* and *abunu* contracts became a dominant contractual arrangement replacing service.

In the Atewa Range, in contrast, cocoa cultivation was taken up in already established settlements, in which the matrilineal segments had already established ownership of land through land clearance. The introduction of cocoa did not involve a movement into new land but the clearance of new areas in which the various matrilineages had settled and the development into new Kwae areas in territories that may have previously been the domain of hunters. Prior to this development women had been the main cultivators of the land, and the menfolk supplemented agriculture with hunting and gold mining. For large parts of the nineteenth century the involvement of men in agriculture was disrupted by warfare and their recruitment into the armies of their overlords. However, men were responsible for clearing land for their wives and providing them with farms on which to nurture crops, weed and provision the household with food. With the introduction of cocoa and evidence of its profitability, men began to enter into cocoa production, clearing larger tracts of land. However, women also participated in cocoa farming. Fathers often provided their daughters with plots of land on which their husbands were expected to develop cocoa farms for them.

In contrast with the migratory Akuapem settlements in which smallholders coexisted with large investors in cocoa, in the Atewa Range settlements, cocoa cultivation was a more pronounced smallholder activity. There were fewer linkages of a service nature between smallholder farmers and large cocoa entrepreneurs and less use of migrant labour. However, the land area into which the peasant cultivators were expanding was rapidly alienated by chiefs. The paramount chief appropriated a considerable area for the creation of the Atewa Range Forest Reserve. This did not take into consideration the needs of the communities surrounding the forest reserve for land for future expansion. The chief of Apinaman also alienated land to migrant farmers. This has created a land shortage which is structured by generation. The grandparent generation started farming at the time of this appropriation and were able to gain sufficient land for farming purposes. However, their children were affected by this appropriation and experienced greater difficulty in gaining land. As a consequence they do not have sufficient land either to farm or pass on to their children and grandchildren. As a result of land shortage and a lack of security in land, in the sense that young people cannot be sure they will get land from their father or mother's brother, participation in family agricultural production becomes increasingly undesirable for youth.

Since this process of land scarcity occurred across generations, women of the grandparent generation were able to acquire significant areas of land for farming. They worked on this land with their daughters and their granddaughters and the land was transmitted as women's property. This property was also used to attract husbands for their daughters, who would work in developing the land. With increasing land shortage women have developed a matrifocal strategy to counter attempts by their brothers to gain hold of this land, arguing that women are the backbone of the matrilineage, and that men erode family property by passing it on to their children who are not members of the matrilineage. This matrifocal ideology is absent at Kofi Pare, where women of the grandparent generation were not able to gain access to significant land in their own right and did not develop female farming work teams. With lack of access to sufficient family land male youth seek to gain land on a sharecropping basis, seek employment in other economic sectors (such as mining and timber), or migrate to other areas.

Apart from the different processes which have resulted in land shortage in the two areas, other economic processes have created similar pressures on the relationship between youth and elders, resulting in a transformation of the agrarian structure. These developments are rooted in the declining world market prices for cocoa, problems of rehabilitating old cocoa plantations, and the movement of migrant labour away from old cocoa production areas, such as the Eastern Region. Local youth have moved in to replace migrant labour, but they are unwilling to accept the annual labour and *abusa* labourer terms on which migrants were hired. They hire themselves out as contract labour or casual daily labour. The hiring of labour became increasingly monetised in the 1970s, in a period of recession in cocoa when farmers had less access to surplus capital. This period of decline also led to a significant movement of youth away from work on family farms, since their elders could no longer cater for their economic and social needs. Apart from casual farm labour, youth moved into sharecropping on the land of non-relatives, augmenting and replacing migrant sharecrop tenants, some of whom had been forced to flee after the Aliens Compliance Order. Others have migrated to the urban areas, and into the informal mining and timber sectors, particularly around the Atewa Range.

Increasing difficulty in getting family youth to work on the family farm and difficulty in paying for hired labour has resulted in growing recourse to sharecropping as a dominant mode of production, in which the land-rich labour-poor landlord hires out land to the land-poor labour-capable tenant in return for a half share of the crop. At Kofi Pare, where cocoa is still an important crop as a result of support from the Cocoa Rehabilitation Project, sharecropping has become a dominant relationship in production, and in some instances fathers are giving out land to sons on a sharecrop basis. However, in the Atewa Range settlements where cocoa is a flagging crop and most farmers are struggling to produce food crops, sharecropping arrangements are not so dominant.

The youth in the Atewa settlements prefer to explore other channels of livelihood to agriculture. As a result of this, it becomes increasingly difficult for farmers to engage in agricultural production. With increasing costs of living, and the capitalisation of social services such as education and health, many farmers are burdened by heavy debts. Unable to gain youth labour or to hire labour, many family elders are increasingly willing to sell land. However, there is not a large demand for land, since most farmers are experiencing problems in agricultural productivity and experiencing shortages in cash flow. A land market has developed but there are few land transactions taking place.

In contrast, at Kofi Pare land is still considered a productive commodity. Farmers prefer to sharecrop land rather than sell it, and there is a large demand for sharecrop tenancies. Land sales are frowned upon and the existence of a land market is not admitted or evident. However, increasing economic hardship forces some people to sell land, and there is a large demand for land. While an open land market does not exist as at Apinaman, more land sales are occurring at Kofi Pare.

Although the Aburi section of Kofi Pare and the Atewa range settlements share a matrilineal kinship system there have been significant differences in the way matriliny is conceptualised and organised in the two areas. This reflects different social relationships between various categories of kin and non-kin constructed around agricultural production, and different organisations of land, labour and capital.

Underlying these differences is a general pattern of a transformation of lineage modes of production and smallholder peasant agriculture and the decline of a service economy based on ties of personal dependence in the face of increasing commodification of life and economic recession. Adults are unable to meet the new needs of children (for social welfare, money, security in employment and land to farm on) yet demand labour services from them. This demand intensifies with economic recession and the decline of cheap migrant labour (originally rooted in colonial attempts to create labour reserves). Parents look to children to fill the vacuum in labour, to replace the labour they cannot afford to hire. But they fail to offer their children security and maintain them. By the age of 13 the children are looking for their own sources of income and alternatives to the agricultural way of life, carrying boards, mining, and migrating to the town markets.

In the present period, with economic liberalisation and expansion of natural resource extraction for exports, the informal mining and timber sectors are particularly attractive to youth. However, the state is also focusing on these economic sectors. Concessions for gold and timber are extending and new regulations are coming in to foster export-oriented growth. These developments are perilous for the youth who frequently find that their livelihood strategies become criminalised by the state, and who become subject to harassment by security forces who round them up from time to time, imprison them or extract payments from them.

This criminalisation of the youth by the state converges with the problems of land-owning elders in organising youth to provide cheap non-monetised labour. Chiefs and elders complain that the youth do not respect their elders any more, lack responsibility, migrate to the urban areas in search of bright lights rather than help their ageing parents on the farm. A moral crusade has been launched in the media against rural youth, who are portrayed as shiftless, disrespectful, drug abusers who need to be imbued with traditional values of respect and moral education. This finds reverberations with the Euro-American obsessions with a contemporary crisis in the family and for youth (drug abuse, teenage pregnancy, street crime, etc.). Structural problems arising from the poverty and immiseration brought on by policies concerned with global market integration, liberalisation, and decline of social welfare expenditure are being attributed to the breakdown of morality within the family (Moore, 1994).

In the Ghanaian context, this concept of a social crisis of youth and the family is by no means new. Dummett (1998:275) recounts that in the late 1880s the chief of Wassa Fiase and his successors "complained to the colonial government that "they could no longer get young men to obey their orders in such matters as the maintenance of public roads and other communal obligations". They appealed to the colonial government to endow them with stronger powers as outlined in the Native Jurisdiction Ordinance of 1883. Allman (1996) reports that during the 1920s, in Asante, chiefs introduced bye-laws which forced women to marry, constructing a discourse based on the decline of family values and female promiscuity. Fortes (1950) also reported on the high incidence of divorce in rural Asante during the 1940s and the difficulty that many men faced in supporting their children.

This analysis has shown that the present inter-generational conflict is not rooted in a moral crisis of youth. It is rooted in conflicts in agricultural production, the components of which include an inability of elders to provide for the present and future needs of youth, and the need for youth to find independent forms of livelihood that remove their labour from the family labour pool. This makes the landholding elders increasingly dependent upon hiring of labour and hiring out of land to tenant sharecrop farmers. The failure to analyse agrarian production within its socioeconomic context and the portrayal of contemporary production problems as a moral problem of youth and family discipline prevents an appropriate analysis of the failings of agricultural development strategies. By promoting the concept of a youth crisis in the state media, the state evades a critique of contemporary policies for rural development and for the development of youth in rural areas.

Chapter 4
Conclusion: Integrating Land and Labour Issues

It is important to conceptualise the land question within the regional economy in which it occurs and within the historical relations of production. The two dominant approaches to the land question in Africa (the evolutionary property rights and communitarian approaches) fail to do this. The first approach conceptualises land in Africa within an evolutionary framework which emphasises security in land through the development of individual property rights. It holds up the owner-operated family farm as the highest evolution of agricultural property. It argues that there is a process of emergence of individual property rights within Africa, and seeks to support this movement. The second approach argues that land administration is characterised by dualism, a modern state sector and a customary sector. Within rural localities customary norms regulate transactions and redistribution of land. At the level of state administration land is managed according to formal and legalistic procedures that are not widely implemented in the countryside. This second approach argues that the modern state framework of land management is not particularly "scientific", "progressive" or "enlightened", as is often the claim of state policy practitioners. These state procedures of land administration are based on colonial prescriptions of land tenure and reflect western notions of property. The lack of recognition of customary forms of land tenure acts as a mechanism to justify and mystify appropriation of land by political elites and their allies. This approach calls for greater recognition of customary land tenure and a role for communities in the administration of land. It argues that African customary principles of land management are dynamic, flexible, and often embody principles of equity and conservation of land for the use of future generations. Thus communities are seen as embodying principles of a moral economy that is sensitive to social redistribution and welfare. This communitarian approach seeks to promote dialogue between communities and the state in the search for forms of land management that respond to popular demands.

These two positions on the land question are not particularly new. They can be traced back to nineteenth century debates on land, between the physiocrats who saw security of private ownership as the essential foundation of the economic order and the position of Henry Maine and John Stuart Mill, that advocate community tenure and the village community. They formed the basis of debates on colonial policy, between imperial constructivism, which favoured the breaking up of communities and the development of new forces of production, and community focussed approaches which advocated building development along natural lines, on a condominium of chiefs and merchant traders. Cowen and 3333333Shenton (1996) argue that the focus on community development in British colonialism begins in 1925 with the publication of the White Paper 'Education Policy in Tropical Africa'. By the 1950s community development was part of state development policy since the concept of community was the means of achieving development. Cowen and Shenton (1996:364) state:

> It was, paradoxically, development doctrine, with its agrarian development and rural enterprise schemes, which fixed population to its given ethnic territory and thereby provided the means by which tribal nationalism could be asserted. Development doctrine had always meant 'more' community and not less of community and there was little that was naturally African about this particular history of development.

The focus on communities and customary institutions is not particularly new. It is the focus on transforming top-down approaches that is new. Top-down approaches refer to the means through which state organisations have attempted to integrate rural dwellers into state development plans. However, by downplaying the role that community institutions have played in development in the colonial phase, communitarians fail to grasp the political economy dimensions of the attempts by states to establish hegemonic control over the rural areas through an alliance with rural class fractions and political elites ("opinion leaders").

In Ghana, during the colonial period a strong tradition of popular organisation developed within communities. These popular organisations represented commoners and youth. They undertook community development schemes, infrastructure programmes, but also stood up for the rights of members against the excesses of chiefs. These organisations played an important part in the anti-colonial movement. Since then, with attainment of independence, most governments have exploited what remains of these popular organisations to further their own interests (Songsore and Denkabe, 1995; Ayee, 1994). Widespread opposition to the system of Native Authorities resulted in reforms to set up elected district councils. However, in the immediate post-independence period the CPP played a prominent role in selecting representatives to these local councils, defeating the objectives of administrative reform (Songsore and Denkabe, 1995). Governments continue to this day to select the executives of district administrations and appoint members to District Assemblies.

In their study of the Upper West Region in Ghana, Songsore and Denkabe (1995) show how popular organisations are coopted by the state. Governments set up their own semi-autonomous mass organisations. These include farmers' organisations, cooperative societies, economic production brigades or 'mobisquads', and regional development projects. They also use local elites to coopt existing organisations, to make sure they represent narrow elite interests allied with the government and not the genuine interests of peasant producers. As a result:

> Organisations at the level of the community, people's organisations, exert hardly any influence in the decision-making process and in planning and implementation of development programmes. .... While grassroots organisations try to reach out without much success to the centre, at various levels with their felt needs and aspirations, the centre, on the other hand, has tended to respond by setting up pseudo-people's organisations in order to control the grassroots and consolidate the social basis of authority (Songsore and Denkabe, 1995:97).

The consequence of these developments is not an absence of community organisation or a lack of integration of community organisations with state organisations, but a cooption of community organisations into state interests, and an identification of the community with the elite interests that are responsible for the process of cooption. In this respect, Wolfe (1994:26) comments:

> Governments began to assign economic and social responsibility to "communities" in the community development programmes that flourished during the 1950s. From that time on, simplistic suppositions that communities are cohesive units that can readily be mobilized to meet these responsibilities have persisted, despite much field research and many programme evaluations demonstrating that the reality is more complex. Membership in the more stable communities, unlike membership in most other local groupings, is not voluntary but depends upon birth or marriage into the community. Communities are made up of people who perpetually negotiate ways of living together. They are rarely egalitarian or given to unlimited reciprocity. Decision-making is more often than not in the hands of a minority able to control key resources, such as land, and which monopolizes the use of violence, usually in alliance with local functionaries of the state. Social peace typically depends on acceptance of the traditional distribution of power and avoidance of issues that might bring conflict out into the open.

An approach to community development and community participation in resource management, which focuses on existing "traditional" authority structures within the community, is likely to enable the coopted minority to continue to represent its interests as those of the community. A communitarian approach which values the role of African communities in development in terms of their capacity to develop institutions that promote consensus and accommodation is likely to enable the minority to impose their programmes on the majority. The underprivileged will be inhibited from articulating positions that may result in conflict, and these will be interpreted by the elite as violations of the customary and community spirit or as backward positions that do not respond to the needs of developing the community in accord with state development plans.

Since a dialogue already exists between the rural elite and the state, inverting what is construed as a top-down approach must involve building variables of social differentiation into the conceptions of popular "community" organisation. Any attempt to continue to represent minorities and traditional authorities as representatives of the communities merely reifies top-down distortions of popular democracy. The weakness of the communitarian position lies in its incapacity to subject the concept of community to critical analysis and to develop a historical and political economic analysis of the nature of the relationship between community organisations and the state from the colonial period, and the impact of this relationship on the peasantry.

The concept of community development may also be inappropriate in the context of the rapid processes of change and transformation occurring in rural society in Africa. A number of recent studies on rural Africa suggest that a structural transformation is occurring in which rural areas are becoming economically more diversified and less dependent upon agriculture. The rural population becomes increasingly mobile and communities lose their social coherence. Economic activities become increasingly individualised and pooling of resources by lineages and domestic units decline (Bryceson, 2000; 1993). At a global level, Wolfe (1994) argues that "stable communities" in which processes of negotiating power and resources continue to be recognised are now becoming exceptional, and rural settlements are becoming increasingly polarised and differentiated as new social networks emerge responding to survival strategies, networks of reciprocity in production and services, and minority cultures of resistance to the dominant development ethics. Wolfe (1994) draws a vivid picture of rural communities in India, in which the landholding elite has divorced itself from the rest of the rural population and has decided to join global society. It travels abroad, sends its children to universities in the city, and watches television programmes from the United States. The middle stratum also looks outside. Unable to go to the United States, its members rely on contract work in the Gulf States. The village poor, unable to subsist on agriculture, are also on the move to cities and towns in search of casual labour. Wolfe (1994) uses the banners "de-localisation of participatory ties" and "de-responsibilisation" to describe these processes of rural dissolution. Bryceson's (2000) banners for these processes are "depeasantisation" and de-agrarianisation".

The processes described by these researchers echo the underlying themes in the Akyem case studies above. The increasing expense of living has placed an increasing burden on social institutions of redistribution within the family. These include the expenses of caring for sick and indigent, for children, non-working youth, and the elderly. These expenses have increased partly as a result of neo-liberal structural adjustment measures, that have attempted to shift the crisis in state management of the economy onto the people. State subsidies of education and health have been removed. Low priorities have been given to providing youth with skills, economic opportunity and employment. Families now have to shoulder the responsibility of catering for youth and providing them with life skills. Meanwhile, the promotion of a global consumer culture and increasing commodification of life result in new wants that cannot be easily satisfied by redistribution mechanisms within lineage systems. Many of the elders within lineages are also experiencing economic uncertainty, declining standards of living and a sense of insecurity. Only a few people are prospering. The elders are also the subject of new pressures of a consumer culture. Bearing the responsibility of families still carries prestige, but prestige can also be gained easily through the path of flaunting the products of global consumer culture.

The elders do not only experience difficulty in meeting the basic needs of their dependants and youth, they also experience difficulty in gaining access to farm labour. The elders do not only fail to meet the basic needs of the youth to negotiate a modern world, they also fail to provide them with the security of access to land to farm. Unable to gain land to farm the youth look for other opportunities outside of agriculture and a process of migration rapidly develops among youth from households with insufficient land to cater for their farming needs. Other youth seek sharecrop contracts or work as casual labour to gain money in the agricultural, and informal mining and timber sectors.

Redistribution mechanisms break down within the lineage and are replaced by reciprocity. The elders give land in the future directly in exchange for labour. The youth serve their elders on the farm and in return their elders promise them bequests of land. But this system is also prone to crisis, as siblings dispute access to land and demand that the land passes to them before going to the next generation. What appears to be an inter-generational conflicts has roots in declining sibling solidarity. Redistribution between sibling groups breaks down, as a result of increasing economic individuation. As a result of this lack of unity, siblings begin to count their own children as separate from the children of their siblings. Unable and unwilling to provide the basic needs of their sisters' children, sisters' children become unwilling to provide farm services for their mother's brother and look to their father to provide for their needs. Men narrow themselves down to providing for their children and children help their fathers on the farm. Fathers bequest their land to their children as gifts. As land becomes scarce, fathers cannot provide for all their children and access to land becomes determined by service on farms. However, the process of fathers granting matrilineal land as gifts to children becomes disputed by others of the father's generation who have access to less land or who have ambitions of controlling larger areas. Reciprocity based on service becomes uncertain. Youth prefer to gain land on a predefined contractual basis, as in sharecropping, rather than through service. Other youth gain a livelihood through casual farm labour. Unable to control the labour of youth the elders are either forced to hire labour or hire land out under sharecrop arrangements (to gain non-monetised labour). An alternative strategy is to sell off land and purchase land as individual property, to break matrilineal interests in the land, to assure children of rights in land, and to lessen obligations to siblings. This strategy also threatens youth, on the basis that their future inheritance is being sold off because of their refusal to provide free farm labour. This enables a new alignment of land holdings to come into being, which become consolidated in the hands of those with capital, irrespective of their social ranking within matrilineal hierarchies.

Through these processes land and labour become increasingly commodified. The elders begin to valorise their control over land as a control over a scarce commodity with market value. The youth begin to valorise their provisions of service in terms of the value of their labour. Since labour markets are more developed than markets in family land, the youth are able to valorise their labour more successfully than the elders, since it is easier to work in alternative labour markets than to sell family land. As the youth withdraw their labour from family circles the family elders begin to accuse the youth of moral misconduct. They depict the youth as lacking respect, as lazy—disliking hard farm work and looking for "quick and easy money", and flighty—moving to the bright lights of the towns to engage in hedonistic activities. However, the elders also play a major role in this process of commodification of family relations, and the youth charge them with being selfish and manipulative.

Through the development of export crop production land acquires a commodity value, which the elders seek to manipulate in their relationship with youth. The basis of family redistribution could never have developed on the basis of the value of land, for this value was always the value of the labour invested within it, in transforming it from a wild state into a farming domain. In the days preceding the expansion of cocoa, the male youth could always clear new uncultivated forest land. The basis of their cooperation with their elders was the support the elders provided them in gaining access to skills and knowledge for gaining a livelihood and negotiating life, and social welfare.

In developing alternative livelihoods, the youth also comes into conflict with the state. Given the weak manufacturing base within the national economy the youth construct their livelihoods around the same natural resources as the state. The most promising informal sector activities that the youth develop focus on the mining and timber sectors. These are the same sectors that the state is giving out as concessions for the development of export-oriented production. As the concession system expands, the economic activities of youth become criminalised. Increasing numbers of youth are picked up by police for engaging in timber and mining activities. The state and state media have rapidly picked up the discourse of elders and village elites, largely through large cocoa farmers (who are in need of cheap labour) on the immorality of youth.

The state combines this discourse with a discourse originating from the United States on the immorality of youth, which includes a concern over drug abuse and teenage pregnancy. However, the global discourse does not originate in issues of farm labour but issues surrounding the dismantling of social welfare. The national discourse mixes its metaphors. Western notions of youth as a category between the ages of 16 and the early twenties become fused with the young men (*mmrant*— who may be 40 years old) of rural farm labour discourse. The causes of lack of youth respect for elders are attributed to lack of moral education and parental control, echoing US moral crusaders.

However, the youth do not suffer from a lack of "moral" education, which is constantly preached to them from the church pulpits and the radio media, but from a lack of access to scientific education. What the state fails to provide for the youth is relevant training and skills and opportunities that will enhance their livelihoods. Youth are unable to complete a basic education because their parents cannot afford the costs of this, and because the state does not in reality provide free basic education, although it claims to make this provision. The quality of education provided in the rural areas is dismal. It fails to reflect the context in which the youth live. It is largely based on rote learning and repetition of empty moral formulas, drawn from old colonial models. The youth are forced to develop their own learning contexts and their networks of social and livelihood learning. They develop their own life skills through informal apprentice systems rather than through formal education. They make use of various mobile networks based on family and craft associations which stretch from the rural setting into urban areas, to gain access to a livelihood.

The state does nothing to further these developments, but points to urban migration as a form of youth decadence. It focuses on introducing policies to encourage youth to remain in the rural areas and in agriculture. Since access to land for agricultural production is limited for the youth, this approach essentially reproduces youth as unskilled agrarian labour. This meets the interests of the main rural clients of the state in the forest zone, wealthy cocoa farmers who need cheap labour.

A second discourse associated with women in rural areas focuses on gender relations. This argues that in today's lean and mean world women suffer from the consequences of men withdrawing their responsibilities towards the matrilineage and focussing on their children. Matrilineal land is becoming scarcer because men are alienating it to their own children. As a consequence, women are suffering from declining access to land and have to rely more on husbands for land. Where marriage is insecure, women suffer from lack of access to land. This discourse argues that women should become the main custodians of matrilineal land. The role of men in the matriliny is ambiguous, since they are divided by loyalties to their wife and children, who do not inherit their matrilineal land, and to their sisters' children who inherit their matrilineal property. In contrast women are not faced with such a contradiction since their children are members of the matriliny. This discourse argues that women can use land more efficiently than men. Men experience difficulty in getting their dependent youth to work for them, while women can get their husbands to work their own land with the ultimate sanction of divorce. This discourse builds upon the solidarity of relations between grandmothers, mothers and daughters in farming and the transmission of women's farm property through this line. It recognises the fragility of marriage as a means through which women can gain access to land. It demands that women should have equal access to family property as men in their own right.

Agriculture is increasingly becoming an individual pursuit. However, contrary to what is claimed by the evolutionary property rights school, this does not take place through the rise of a nuclear family with its neatly bounded family farm. The pressures that erode lineage families also erode household relations. The lineage is not a structure that looms over nuclear families, sapping their vitality and redistributing their wealth. The lineage family has existed in the past because of the difficulty that other production and consumption units experienced in reproducing themselves. Meillassoux (1978:326) comments:

> Kinship relations acted as the relations of production. They corresponded to a social organisation of production which made the labour of each person inseparable from that of all of them. They fitted a system of redistribution which allowed the apportioning of the common product among all the members of the group according to their needs rather than their labour. In order to maintain the functional balance of the unit, kinship relations extended beyond strict blood relations. In the absence of specialisation and exchange wealth had only a conventional value and its social use was inseparable from the rank of its possessor.

The breakdown of systems of redistribution does not only result in men not providing for kin other than their biological kin, but also men not being able to support their own biological kin. In this situation, children and women who would have been looked after by a benefactor who would be a prominent elder within the lineage, now have to fend for themselves. The breakdown in the lineage results in various types of fragmented households coming into being. Youth begin to fend for themselves from an early age, hiring out their labour and migrating to towns in search of casual work or to engage in petty trading. Different interests within the household begin to exert their own interests. These manifest themselves as struggles between elders and youth and men and women. However, these categories are symbolic of new relations and new organisations that are developing within the rural areas. The lineage as an organisation redistributing wealth, land and labour services within specific community localities is replaced by more amorphous and mobile networks of bilateral kinship extending over large areas of towns, villages and cities. These networks become the focus of livelihood strategies through which people find work, sustenance, support, education and training for their children, and develop economic ventures.

New types of associations also begin to develop which reflect attempts to create new livelihoods and support structures for these livelihoods. These often take the form of craft and trade associations that develop in particular localities in which artisans and traders congregate. The association develops to help members with production problems, but also takes on social support functions, taking responsibility for helping its members organise funerals, meet medical expenditures, etc. These associations are frequently urban based or focussed on particular localities. In Accra there are several artisan associations which have developed among youth practising particular crafts. The artisans in these associations often originate from common areas in the rural hinterland and they migrated to the city because of land shortage and limited agricultural opportunities.

For instance, around Switchback Road in Accra, near the Department of Parks and Gardens, can be found a group of cane weavers who have formed the Unity Cane Weavers Association. They have about 60 members in their association. They originate from Enyiresi in northern Akyem Abuakwa Region. In this area youth began weaving baskets from rattan in the 1950s when they began to experience land shortage. They learned the art of rattan weaving from youth in the Asamankese area. As cane became scarce they began to move to new areas in search of cane. Eventually they relocated to Accra and expanded into rattan cane furniture production. The rattan they used was supplied by specialised gatherers who moved from the Eastern Region into the Western Region. They eventually came together to form the Rattan Suppliers Association, which established its headquarters at the Railways in Accra, before relocating to the Motorway Extension where most rattan weavers are situated.

Similarly, up in the Akuapem Hills, at Aburi, can be found large numbers of woodcarvers, who have formed an association known as the Aburi Industrial Centre. The origins of this association go back to 1983, following the mass deportation of Ghanaians working in Nigeria. Many youth returned to Aburi, where they found little scope for acquiring land to go into farming. Two old men were carving wood under a tree. With nothing else to do some of the repatriated youth began to learn woodcarving. As they began to gain experience in the craft they took on apprentices. Later on, a reverend minister in the area began to organise a vocational training centre around this woodcraft base, introducing tailoring, dressmaking, and carpentry. He gained some German funding for the project, which became known

as the Aburi Industrial Centre. None of the other crafts introduced with-
stood the test of time, and the Aburi Industrial Centre eventually settled
down as a woodworking craft workshop based on an apprentice system.
The Aburi Industrial Centre currently has about 600 members, including
apprentices. Members pay dues and elect an executive membership. The
Aburi Industrial Centre has also affiliated itself to the Informal Sector of the
Timber and Woodworkers Union, joining a network of chainsaw operators,
carpenters and canoe carvers. Some of the woodcarvers trained at Aburi
have moved to other localities to establish or join newly developing workshops. Between Adeiso and Asamankese, several woodcarving centres are
developing, specialising in mortar carving and drums.

In developing their crafts these associations experience difficulty in gaining access to raw materials. This results from conservation policies introduced by the Forestry Service. These conservation measures are largely
developed to protect export timber interests in addition to forests, but introduce procedures which affect users of non-timber species. The procedures
for the exploitation of trees in relationship to craft production are not clear
and transparent, resulting in constant harassment of providers of raw materials for artisan production and the collection of fees for passage by police
and customs officials. Recent attempts at developing community participation in forest management also adversely affects craft producers. This seeks
to secure the non-timber forest products within forest reserves for the surrounding forest-edge communities against outsiders who are portrayed as
rapaciously harvesting resources in which they have no long-term interest.
Long-term interest is equated with sedentary populations who live around
the resource. In reality, rural sedentary farming communities cannot exploit
these resources for livelihood opportunities, since this is a full time occupation, requiring considerable market information and organisational ability.
The development of these urban-based mobile networks resulted precisely
from the constraints that artisans experienced in attempting to develop
these resources within rural communities. They were eventually forced to
reorganise and relocate to centres near the main urban markets.

It is increasingly becoming apparent that a period of rapid transformation is taking place in rural areas. The export crop and food crop production
base can no longer sustain the rural population and new sectors are coming
into being. This results in a labour crisis for the many farmers who depend
upon hired labour. Labour becomes increasingly expensive, because it has to
compete with labour in other sectors including the urban informal service
sectors and rural non-agricultural labour. These sectors provide livelihood
opportunities for youth who are no longer willing to provide a free labour
service for their elders on their farms. Cheap long distance migrant labour is
also not available since it has long since moved out of Ghana to more profit-
able sectors elsewhere. Faced with increasing costs of labour the big cocoa
farmers and landowners look back to the early colonial period when labour

was cheap, and in the name of tradition call upon government to introduce policies to contain the movement of youth and instil traditional moral and cultural values within the youth.

A focus on community management of land based on custom or tradition, directly supports the interests of the large landowners and elders. In developing structures for the community management of land along customary lines, the interests of landowning elders will be furthered. A focus on community management of land will not enhance the position of those who do not have access to sufficient land for farming or control over land. Mobile networks of producers using natural resources outside of agriculture are unlikely to gain secure rights to their resources since they are not recognised within the framework of community land rights.

This study shows that the role of matrilineages in the management of land has been breaking down and is in a process of transformation. The right of elders to control land on the basis of tradition is being challenged because their role in redistributing wealth has broken down. The matrifocal ideology challenges the authority of elders to distribute matrilineal land because they no longer shoulder the responsibility of the matrilineage. It argues that women have now become the heirs to social cohesion with the matrilineal family. The youth withdraw their labour from the leaders because the elders do not provide them with the means for a secure future. The matrilineage will not be able to reproduce itself in the future as a farming entity, as a corporate group controlling agricultural property, since it is unable to organise family labour. Thus, approaches which stress traditional organisations in the management of land are misplaced and backward looking.

The future lies with the youth. Therefore, progress lies in creating conditions for them to develop their aspirations, and the means to realise the goals that they set. Sadly, lessons which were learnt in the 1950s with the dismembering of Indirect Rule have been forgotten.

The future structure of rural production relations is not, as yet, clear. More research needs to be undertaken on new types of mobile rural organisations, associations and networks which are coming into being and their related production bases.

The land question cannot be abstracted from the labour question and the problems of social redistribution and welfare. The future of the rural areas and their regeneration will not largely depend upon the creation of security in land but on creating security for the youth and opportunities for them to gain new skills to create new livelihood openings. The future lies in creating new economic sectors outside staple exports and food products which will create opportunities for people without access to land. It lies in promoting mobility within rural areas and between the rural and the urban areas, and in promoting information exchange and a new type of education. These developments will create greater economic security. This will bring about

greater land security in the rural areas, as land becomes one economic resource among many, rather than a means of gaining monopoly control over
rural labour.

References

Addo, N.O. (1972) "Employment and Labour Supply on Ghana's Cocoa Farms in the Pre- and Post-Aliens Compliance Order Era", *The Economic Bulletin of Ghana*, 2(4):33–50.

Addo-Fenning, R. (1997) *Akyem Abuakwa 1700–1943: From Ofori Panin to Sir Ofori Atta*. Trondheim: Department of History, Norwegian University of Science and Technology.

Addo-Fening, R. (1974) "The Asamankese Dispute 1919–34", in *Akyem Abuakwa and the Politics of the Inter-War Period in Ghana*, Mittelungen der Basler Afrika Bibliographien, 12:61–89.

Adomako Safo, J. (1974) "The Effects of the Expulsion of Migrant Workers in Ghana's Economy, with Particular Reference to the Cocoa Industry", in S. Amin (ed.), *Modern Migrations in West Africa*. London: International African Institute.

Allman, J. (1996) "Rounding up Spinsters: Gender chaos and unmarried women in colonial Asante", *Journal of African History*, 37:195–214.

Amankwah, H.A. (1989) *The Legal Regime of Land Use in West Africa: Ghana and Nigeria*. Tasmania: Pacific Law Press, Hobart.

Amanor, K.S. (1998) "Structural Adjustment and the changing political economy of land in West Africa", paper presented at Synthesis Conference on Structural Adjustment and Socio-Economic Change in Sub-Saharan Africa at Center for Development Studies, Copenhagen 3–5 December.

Amanor, K.S. (1994) *The New Frontier: Farmers' responses to land degradation*, London: Zed Press; and Geneva: UNRISD.

Amanor, K.S. with M. Kude Diderutuah (2000) "Land and Labour Contracts in the Oil Palm and Citrus Belt of Ghana", paper presented at IIED and GRET Workshop on June 2–6, Ouagadougou.

Amin, S. (1972) "Underdevelopment and Dependence in Black Africa: Origins and contemporary forms", *Journal of Modern African Studies*, Vol 10(4):503–24.

Asad, T. (1979) "Anthropology and the Analysis of Ideology", *Man* (NS) 14:607–27.

Ayee, J.R.A. (1994) *An Anatomy of Public Policy Implementation: The case of decentralization policies in Ghana*. Aldershot: Avebury.

Barth, F. (1967) "Economic Spheres in Darfur", in R. Firth (ed.), *Themes in Economic Anthropology*. London: Tavistock.

Beckett, W.H. (1947) *Akokoaso: A Survey of a Gold Coast Village*. Monographs on Social Anthropology No 10. London: Percy Lund, Humphries and Co. for London School of Economics.

Berry, S. (1993) *No Condition Is Permanent: The Social Dynamics of Agrarian Change in Sub-Sahara Africa*. Madison: University of Wisconsin Press.

Brandão, A.S.P. and G. Feder (1995) "Regulatory policies and reform: The case of land markets", in C. Frischtak (ed.), *Regulatory Policies and Reform: A Comparative Perspective*. Washington: World Bank, pp. 191–209.

Bruce, J.W. (1993) "Do Indigenous Tenure Systems Constrain Agricultural Development?", in T.J. Basset and D.E. Crummey (eds), *Land in African Agrarian Systems*. Madison: University of Wisconsin Press, pp. 35–56.

Bryceson, D. (2000) *Rural Africa at the Crossroads: Livelihood practices and policies*. ODI Natural Resource Perspectives no 52. London: ODI.

Bryceson, D. (1993) *De-Agrarianization and Rural Employment Generation in Sub-Saharan Africa: Process and Prospects*. African Studies Centre Working Paper Vol. 19. Leiden: Afrika-Studiecentrum.

Carter, M. and F. Zimmerman (1993) *Risk, Scarcity and Land Market: The uneven economics of, induced institutional change in the West African Sahel*. Working Paper No. 86, Center for Institutional Reform and the Informal Sector, University of Maryland at College Park.

Cowen, M.P. and R.W. Shenton (1996) *Doctrines of Development*. London: Routledge.

Coussey Commission (1949) *Report to his Excellency the Governor by the Committee on Constitutional Reform*. Secretary of State of the Colonies, British Parliamentary Papers, cmd no 248.

Danquah, J.B. (1928a) *Akan Laws and Custom*. London: Routledge and Sons.

Danquah, J.B. (1928b) *Cases in Akan Law*. London: Routledge and Sons.

Danquah, J.B. (1928c) *An Epistle to the Educated Youngman in Akim Abuakwa*. Accra.

Deininger, K. and H. Binswanger (1998) *The Evolution of the World Bank's Land Policy*. On net, worldbank.org.

Douglas, M. (1969) "Is Matriliny Doomed in Africa?", in M. Douglas and P.M. Kaberry (eds), *Man in Africa*. London: Tavistock Publishing, pp. 121–135.

Dummett, R. (1998) *El Dorado in West Africa: The gold mining frontier, African labour and colonial capitalism in the Gold Coast, 1875–1900*. Athens: Ohio University Press and London: James Curry.

Dubois, O. (1997) *Rights and Wrongs to Land and Forest Resources in sub-Saharan Africa: Bridging the gap between customary and formal rules*. Forest Participation Series No. 10. London: IIED.

Dupré, G. and P.P. Rey (1978) "Reflections on the Relevance of a Theory of the History of Exchange", in D. Seddeon (ed.), *Relations of Production: Marxist approaches to economic anthropology*. London: Frank Cass, pp. 171–208. Originally published as "Reflexions sur la pertinence d'une théorie des échanges" in *Cahiers Internationaux de Sociologie*, 2(2) 1973:133–62.

Egbe, S. (1996) "Forest Tenure and Access to Forest Resources in Cameroon: An overview", in *Managing Land Tenure and Resource Access in West Africa: Proceedings of a Regional Workshop*, Gorée, Senegal, November 18–22, 1966, convened by L'Université de Saint-Louis, GRET, IIED, Ministère Français de la Coopération and British Overseas Development Administration, London, pp. 16–34.

Fayorsey, C. (1995) "Ga Women's Autonomy: A critique of the concepts and economy of household and family", *African Anthropology*, 2(1):91–130.

Feder, G. and D. Feeny (1991) "Land Tenure and Property Rights: Theory and Implications for Development Policy", *World Bank Economic Review*, 5:135–53.

Field, M.J. (1948) *Akim Kotoku: An oman of the Gold Coast*. London: Crown Agents.

Field, M.J. (1943) "The Agricultural System of the Manya Krobo of the Gold Coast", *Africa*, Vol 14:54–65.

Fortes, M. (1969) *Kinship and the Social Order*. London: Routledge and Kegan Paul.

Fortes, M. (1950) "Kinship and Marriage among the Ashanti", in A.R. Radcliffe-Brown and D. Forde (eds), *African Systems of Kinship and Marriage*. London: Oxford University Press, pp. 252–84.

Goody, J. (1959) "The Mother's Brother and the Sister's Son in West Africa", *Journal of the Royal Anthropological Institute*, 89(1):61–86.

Hill, P. (1970) *Rural Capitalism in West Africa*. Cambridge: Cambridge University Press.

Hill, P. (1963) *The Migrant Cocoa-Farmers of Southern Ghana: A study in rural capitalism*. Cambridge: Cambridge University Press.

Hill, P. (1956) *The Gold Coast Cocoa Farmer*. London: Oxford University Press.

Hill, P. and C. McGlade (1957) *An Economic Survey of Cocoa Farmers in Northern Akim Abuakwa*. Cocoa Research Series no.1. Economic Research Division, University College of Ghana.

Hunter, J.M. (1963) "Cocoa Migrations and Patterns of Land Ownership in the Densu Valley near Suhum, Ghana", *Transactions and Papers of the Institute of British Geographers*, Vol. 33:161–86.

Johnson, M. (1964) "Migrants Progress", Part 1, *Bulletin of the Ghana Geographical Society*, 9(2):4–27.

Johnson, M. (1965) "Migrants Progress", Part 2, *Bulletin of the Ghana Geographical Society*, 10(2):13–40.

Kasanga, K. (1996) "Land Tenure, Resource Access and Decentralization: The political economy of land tenure in Ghana", in *Managing Land Tenure and Resource Access in West Africa: Proceedings of a Regional Workshop*, Gorée, Senegal, November 18–22, 1966, convened by L'Université de Saint-Louis, GRET, IIED, Ministère Français de la Coopération and British Overseas Development Administration, London, pp. 84–106.

Kea, R.A. (1982) *Settlements, Trade, and Polities in the Seventeenth Century Gold Coast*. Baltimore: John Hopkins.

Konings, P. (1986) *The State and Rural Class Formation in Ghana*. London: Routledge and Kegan Paul.

Lavigne Delville, P. (2000) "Harmonising Formal Law and Customary Land Rights in French-Speaking West Africa", in C. Toulmin and J. Quan (eds), *Evolving land rights, policy and tenure in Africa*. London: IIED, NRI and DFID, pp. 97–122.

Lavigne Delville, P. (1998) *Rural Land Tenure, Renewable Natural Resources and Development in Africa: Comparative analysis of different approaches*. Paris: Ministère des Affaires Étrangères-Coopération et Francophone.

Levtzion, N. (2000) "Islam in Bilad al-Sudan to 1800", in N. Levtzion and R.L. Pouwels (eds), *The History of Islam in Africa*. Athens: Ohio University Press; London: James Currey; South Africa: David Philip.

MacKenzie, F. (1993) "'A Piece of Land Never Shrinks': Reconceptualizing land tenure in a smallholding district, Kenya", in T.J Basset and D.E. Crummey (eds), *Land in African Agrarian Systems*. Madison: University of Wisconsin Press, pp. 194–221.

Macmillan, W.M. (1946) "African Development", in C.K. Meek, W.M. Macmillan and E.R.J. Hussey, *Europe and West Africa: Some problems of adjustment*. London: Oxford University Press.

Meek, C.K. (1946) *Land Law and Custom in the Colonies*. Oxford: Oxford University Press.

Meillassoux, C. (1978) "Kinship Relations and Relations of Production", in D. Seddon (ed.), *Relations of Production: Marxist approaches to economic history*. London: Frank Cass, pp. 289–330.

Meillassoux, C. (1972) *Anthropologie économique des Gouro de Côte d'Ivoire: de l'économique de subsistance à l'agriculture commerciale*. Paris: Mouton.

Meillassoux, C. ed. (1971) *The Development of Indigenous Trade and Markets in West Africa*. London: Oxford University Press.

Meillassoux, C. (1964) *Anthropologie économique des Gouro de Côte d'Ivoire; de l'économie de subsistance à l'agriculture commerciale*. Paris: Mouton.

Moore, H. (1994) *Is there a crisis in the family?* Occasional Paper no. 3, World Summit for Social Development. Geneva: UNRISD.

Murdock, G.P. (1949) *Social Structure*. New York: Macmillan.

Okali, C. (1983) *Cocoa and Kinship in Ghana: The matrilineal Akan of Ghana*. London: Kegan Paul.

Okoth-Ogendo, H.W.O. (1994) "Land Tenure, Agrarian Legislation and Environmental Management Systems", in R.J. Bakema (ed.), *Land Tenure and Sustainable Land Use*. Bulletin 332. Amsterdam: Royal Tropical Institute, pp. 21–30.

Parkin, D. (1972) *Palms, wine and witnesses: Public spirit and private gain in an African community*. San Francisco, London and Toronto: Chandler Publishing Company.

Platteau, J.-P. (2000) "Does Africa Need Land Reform", in C. Toulmin and J. Quan (eds), *Evolving land rights, policy and tenure in Africa*. IIED, NRI and DFID, London, p.51–74.

Rathbone, R. (1993) *Murder and Politics in Colonial Ghana*. New Haven and London: Yale University Press.

Rathbone, R. (1996) "Defining Akyemfo: The construction of citizenship in Akyem Abuakwa, Ghana, 1700–1939", *Africa*, 66(4):506–25.

Richards, A. (1950) "Some Types of Family Structure among the Central Bantu", in A.R. Radcliffe-Brown and D. Forde (eds), *African Systems of Kinship and Marriage*. London: Oxford University Press, pp. 207–51.

Rosenzweig, M.R., and Binswanger, H.P. (1993) "Wealth, weather risk and the composition and profitability of agricultural investments", *Economic Journal*, 103:56–58.

Rouch, J. (1954) *Notes on Migrations into the Gold Coast*. Paris: Musée de l'Homme.

Simensen, J. (1975) *Commoners, Chiefs and Colonial Government: British policy and local politics in Akyem Abuakwa, Ghana, under Colonial Rule*, unpubished PhD thesis, University of Trondheim.

Simensen, J. (1974) "Crisis in Akyem Abuakwa: The Native Administration Revenue Measure of 1932", in *Akyem Abuakwa and the Politics of the Inter-War Period in Ghana*, Mittelungen der Basler Afrika Bibliographien, 12:90–102.

Skinner, E.P. (1965) "Labor Migrations among the Mossi of the Upper Volta", in H. Kuper (ed.), *Urbanisation and Migration in West Africa*. Berkeley, CA: University of California Press.

Smith, R. T. (1996) *The Matrifocal Family*. London: Routledge.

Smith, R. T. (1973) "The Matrifocal Family", in J. Goody (ed.), *The Character of Kinship*. London: Cambridge University Press, pp. 121–44.

Songsore, J. (1983) *Intra-regional and Interregional Labour Migrations in Historical Perspective: The example of N.W. Ghana*. Occasional Paper no. 17, University of Port Harcourt, Faculty of Social Science.

Songsore, J. and A. Denkabe (1995) *Challenging Rural Poverty in Northern Ghana: The case of the Upper-West Region*. Trondheim: Centre for Environment and Development, University of Trondheim.

Thomas, R.G. (1973) "Forced Labour in British West Africa: The case of the Northern Territories of the Gold Coast 1906–1927", *Journal of African History*, 14(1):78–103.

Toulmin, C. and J. Quan (2000) "Evolving Land Rights, Tenure and Policy in Sub-Saharan Africa", in C. Toulmin and J. Quan (eds), *Evolving land rights, policy and tenure in Africa*, IIED, NRI and DFID, London, pp. 1–30.

Watts, M.J. (1993) "Idioms of Land and Labour: Producing politics and rice in Senegambia", in T.J Basset and D.E. Crummey (eds), *Land in African Agrarian Systems*. Madison: University of Wisconsin Press, pp. 157–93.

Wilks, I.G. (1993) *Forests of Gold: Essays on the Akan and the kingdom of Asante*. Athens: Ohio University Press.

Wilks, I.G. (1982) "The State of the Akan and the Akan State: A discussion", *Cahiers d'Etudes Africaines*, Vol 22(3&4):231–49.

Wilks, I.G. (1977) "Land, labour and capital and the Forest Kingdom of Asante", in J. Friedman and M.J. Rowlands (eds), *The Evolution of Social Systems*. Institute of Archaelogy, University of London.

Wilks, I.G. (1958) *Akwamu 1650–1750: A study of the rise and fall of a West African empire*, MA thesis, University of Wales.

Wolfe, M. (1994) *Social Integration: Institutions and actors*. Geneva: UNRISD.

Wolfson, F. (1953) "A Price Agreement on the Gold Coast—the Krobo Oil Boycott 1858–1860", *The Economic History Review*, 6:68–77.

Publications of the research programme "Political and Social Context of Structural Adjustment in Africa" published by the Nordic Africa Institute

Gibbon P., Bangura and A. Ofstad (eds.), 1992, *Authoritarianism, Democracy and Adjustment. The Politics of Economic Reform in Africa.* Seminar proceedings no. 26.

Gibbon, P. (ed.), 1993, *Social Change and Economic Reform in Africa.*

Chachage, C.S.L., M. Ericsson and P. Gibbon, 1993, *Mining and Structural Adjustment. Studies on Zimbabwe and Tanzania.* Research report no. 92.

Neocosmos, M., 1993, *The Agrarian Question in Africa and the Concept of "Accumulation from Below". Economics and Politics in the Struggle for Democracy.* Research report no. 93.

Kanyinga. K., A.S.Z. Kiondo and P. Tidemand, 1994, *The New Local Level Politics in East Africa. Studies on Uganda, Tanzania and Kenya.* Edited and introduced by Peter Gibbon. Research report no. 95.

Osaghae, E.E., 1995, *Structural Adjustment and Ethnicity in Nigeria.* Research report no. 98.

Gibbon, P. (ed.), 1995, *Markets, Civil Society and Democracy in Kenya.*

Gibbon P. (ed.), 1995, *Structural Adjustment and the Working Poor in Zimbabwe.*

Gibbon, P., 1995, *Liberalised Development in Tanzania.*

Bijlmakers. L.A., M.T. Bassett and D.M. Sanders, 1996, *Health and Structural Adjustment in Rural and Urban Zimbabwe.* Research report no. 101.

Gibbon, P. and A.O. Olukoshi, 1996, *Structural Adjustment and Socio-Economic Change in Sub-Saharan Africa. Some Conceptual, Methodological and Research Issues.* Research report no. 102.

Olukoshi. A.O. and L. Laakso (eds.), 1996, *Challenges to the Nation-State in Africa.*

Olukoshi, A.O. (ed.), 1998, *The Politics of Opposition in Contemporary Africa.*

Egwu, S.G., 1998, *Structural Adjustment, Agrarian Change and Rural Ethnicity in Nigeria.* Research report no. 103.

Olukoshi, A.O., 1998, *The Elusive Prince of Denmark. Structural Adjustment and the Crisis of Governance in Africa.* Research report no. 104.

Bijlmakers. L.A., M.T. Bassett and D.M. Sanders, 1998, *Socioeconomic Stress, Health and Child Nutritional Status in Zimbabwe at a Time of Economic Structural Adjustment. A Three Year Longitudinal Study.* Research report no. 105.

Mupedziswa, R. and P. Gumbo, 1998, *Structural Adjustment and Women Informal Sector Traders in Harare, Zimbabwe.* Research report no. 106.

Chiwele, D.K., P. Muyatwa-Sipula and H. Kalinda, 1998, *Private Sector Response to Agricultural Marketing Liberalisation in Zambia. A Case Study of Eastern Province Maize Markets.* Research report no. 107.

Amanor, K.S., 1999, *Global Restructuring and Land Rights in Ghana. Forest Food Chains, Timber and Rural Livelihoods.* Research report no. 108.

Ongile, G.A., 1999, *Gender and Agricultural Supply Responses to Structural Adjustment Programmes. A Case Study of Smallholder Tea Producers in Kericho, Kenya.* Research report no. 109.

Sachikonye, Lloyd M., 1999, *Restructuring or De-Industrializing? Zimbabwe's Textile and Metal Industries under Adjustment.* Research report no. 110.

Gaidzanwa, Rudo, 1999, *Voting with their Feet. Zimbabwean Nurses and Doctors in the Era of Structural Adjustment*. Research report no. 111.

Hashim, Yahaya and Kate Meagher, 1999, *Cross-Border Trade and the Parallel Currency Market—Trade and Finance in the Context of Structural Adjustment. A Case Study from Kano, Nigeria*. Research report no. 113.

Moyo, Sam, 2000, *Land Reform under Structural Adjustment in Zimbabwe. Land Use Change in the Mashonaland Provinces*.

Jega, Attahiru (ed.), 2000, *Identity Transformation and Identity Politics under Structural Adjustment in Nigeria*.

Kanyinga, Karuti, 2000, *Re-Distribution from Above. The Politics of Land Rights and Squatting in Coastal Kenya*. Research report no. 115.

Amanor, Kojo Sebastian, 2001, *Land, Labour and the Family in Souhtern Ghana. A Critique of Land Policy under Neo-Liberalisation*. Research report no. 116.

Research Reports published by the Institute

Some of the reports are out of print. Photocopies of these reports can be obtained at a cost of SEK 0:50/page.

1. Meyer-Heiselberg, Richard, *Notes from Liberated African Department in the Archives at Fourah Bay College, Freetown, Sierra Leone.* 61 pp. 1967 (OUT-OF-PRINT)

2. Not published.

3. Carlsson, Gunnar, *Benthonic Fauna in African Watercourses with Special Reference to Black Fly Populations.* 13 pp. 1968 (OUT-OF-PRINT)

4. Eldblom, Lars, *Land Tenure—Social Organiza tion and Structure.* 18 pp. 1969 (OUT-OF-PRINT)

5. Bjerén, Gunilla, *Makelle Elementary School Drop-Out. 1967.* 80 pp. 1969 (OUT-OF-PRINT)

6. Møberg, Jens Peter, *Report Concerning the Soil Profile Investigation and Collection of Soil Samples in the West Lake Region of Tanzania.* 44 pp. 1970 (OUT-OF-PRINT)

7. Selinus, Ruth, *The Traditional Foods of the Central Ethiopian Highlands.* 34 pp. 1971 (OUT-OF-PRINT)

8. Hägg, Ingemund, *Some State-Controlled Industrial Companies in Tanzania. A Case Study.* 18 pp. 1971 (OUT-OF-PRINT)

9. Bjerén, Gunilla, *Some Theoretical and Methodological Aspects of the Study of African Urbanization.* 38 pp. 1971 (OUT-OF-PRINT)

10. Linné, Olga, *An Evaluation of Kenya Science Teacher's College.* 67 pp. 1971. SEK 45,-

11. Nellis, John R., *Who Pays Tax in Kenya?* 22 pp. 1972. SEK 45,-

12. Bondestam, Lars, *Population Growth Control in Kenya.* 59 pp. 1972 (OUT OF PRINT)

13. Hall, Budd L., *Wakati Wa Furaha. An Evaluation of a Radio Study Group Campaign.* 47 pp. 1973. SEK 45,-

14. Ståhl, Michael, *Contradictions in Agricultural Development. A Study of Three Minimum Package Projects in Southern Ethiopia.* 65 pp. 1973 (OUT-OF-PRINT)

15. Linné, Olga, *An Evaluation of Kenya Science Teachers College. Phase II 1970–71.* 91 pp. 1973 (OUT-OF-PRINT)

16. Lodhi, Abdulaziz Y., *The Institution of Slavery in Zanzibar and Pemba.* 40 pp. 1973. ISBN 91-7106-066-9 (OUT-OF-PRINT)

17. Lundqvist, Jan, *The Economic Structure of Morogoro Town. Some Sectoral and Regional Characteristics of a Medium-Sized African Town.* 70 pp. 1973. ISBN 91-7106-068-5 (OUT-OF-PRINT)

18. Bondestam, Lars, *Some Notes on African Statistics. Collection, Reliability and Interpretation.* 59 pp. 1973. ISBN 91-7106-069-4 (OUT-OF-PRINT)

19. Jensen, Peter Føge, *Soviet Research on Africa. With Special Reference to International Relations.* 68 pp. 1973. ISBN 91-7106-070-7 (OUT-OF-PRINT)

20. Sjöström, Rolf & Margareta, *YDLC—A Literacy Campaign in Ethiopia. An Introductory Study and a Plan for Further Research.* 72 pp. 1973. ISBN 91-7106-071-5 (OUT-OF-PRINT)

21. Ndongko, Wilfred A., *Regional Economic Planning in Cameroon.* 21 pp. 1974. SEK 45,-. ISBN 91-7106-073-1

22. Pipping-van Hulten, Ida, *An Episode of Colonial History: The German Press in Tanzania 1901–1914.* 47 pp. 1974. SEK 45,-. ISBN 91-7106-077-4

23. Magnusson, Åke, *Swedish Investments in South Africa.* 57 pp. 1974. SEK 45,-. ISBN 91-7106-078-2

24. Nellis, John R., *The Ethnic Composition of Leading Kenyan Government Positions.* 26 pp. 1974. SEK 45,-. ISBN 91-7106-079-0

25. Francke, Anita, *Kibaha Farmers' Training Centre. Impact Study 1965–1968.* 106 pp. 1974. SEK 45,-. ISBN 91-7106-081-2

26. Aasland, Tertit, *On the Move-to-the-Left in Uganda 1969–1971.* 71 pp. 1974. SEK 45,-. ISBN 91-7106-083-9

27. Kirk-Greene, Anthony H.M., *The Genesis of the Nigerian Civil War and the Theory of Fear.* 32 pp. 1975. SEK 45,-. ISBN 91-7106-085-5

28. Okereke, Okoro, *Agrarian Development Pro grammes of African Countries. A Reappraisal of Problems of Policy.* 20 pp. 1975. SEK 45,-. ISBN 91-7106-086-3

29. Kjekshus, Helge, *The Elected Elite. A Socio-Economic Profile of Candidates in Tanzania's Parliamentary Election, 1970.* 40 pp. 1975. SEK 45,-. ISBN 91-7106-087-1

30. Frantz, Charles, *Pastoral Societies, Stratification and National Integration in Africa.* 34 pp. 1975. ISBN 91-7106-088-X (OUT OF PRINT)

31. Esh, Tina & Illith Rosenblum, *Tourism in Developing Countries—Trick or Treat? A Report from the Gambia.* 80 pp. 1975. ISBN 91-7106-094-4 (OUT-OF-PRINT)

32. Clayton, Anthony, *The 1948 Zanzibar General Strike.* 66 pp. 1976. ISBN 91-7106-094-4 (OUT OF PRINT)

33. Pipping, Knut, *Land Holding in the Usangu Plain. A Survey of Two Villages in the Southern Highlands of Tanzania.* 122 pp. 1976. ISBN 91-7106-097-9 (OUT OF PRINT)

34. Lundström, Karl Johan, *North-Eastern Ethiopia: Society in Famine. A Study of Three Social*

Institutions in a Period of Severe Strain. 80 pp. 1976. ISBN 91-7106-098-7 (OUT-OF-PRINT)

35. Magnusson, Åke, The Voice of South Africa. 55 pp. 1976. ISBN 91-7106-106-1 (OUT OF PRINT)

36. Ghai, Yash P., Reflection on Law and Economic Integration in East Africa. 41 pp. 1976. ISBN 91-7106-105-3 (OUT-OF-PRINT)

37. Carlsson, Jerker, Transnational Companies in Liberia. The Role of Transnational Companies in the Economic Development of Liberia. 51 pp. 1977. SEK 45,-. ISBN 91-7106-107-X

38. Green, Reginald H., Toward Socialism and Self Reliance. Tanzania's Striving for Sustained Transition Projected. 57 pp. 1977. ISBN 91-7106-108-8 (OUT-OF-PRINT)

39. Sjöström, Rolf & Margareta, Literacy Schools in a Rural Society. A Study of Yemissrach Dimts Literacy Campaign in Ethiopia. 130 pp. 1977. ISBN 91-7106-109-6 (OUT-OF-PRINT)

40. Ståhl, Michael, New Seeds in Old Soil. A Study of the Land Reform Process in Western Wollega, Ethiopia 1975–76. 90 pp. 1977. SEK 45,-. ISBN 91-7106-112-6

41. Holmberg, Johan, Grain Marketing and Land Reform in Ethiopia. An Analysis of the Marketing and Pricing of Food Grains in 1976 after the Land Reform. 34 pp. 1977. ISBN 91-7106-113-4 (OUT-OF-PRINT)

42. Egerö, Bertil, Mozambique and Angola: Reconstruction in the Social Sciences. 78 pp. 1977. ISBN 91-7106-118-5 (OUT OF PRINT)

43. Hansen, H. B., Ethnicity and Military Rule in Uganda. 136 pp. 1977. ISBN 91-7106-118-5 (OUT-OF-PRINT)

44. Bhagavan, M.R., Zambia: Impact of Industrial Strategy on Regional Imbalance and Social Inequality. 76 pp. 1978. ISBN 91-7106-119-3 (OUT OF PRINT)

45. Aaby, Peter, The State of Guinea-Bissau. African Socialism or Socialism in Africa? 35 pp. 1978. ISBN 91-7106-133-9 (OUT-OF-PRINT)

46. Abdel-Rahim, Muddathir, Changing Patterns of Civilian-Military Relations in the Sudan. 32 pp. 1978. ISBN 91-7106-137-1 (OUT-OF-PRINT)

47. Jönsson, Lars, La Révolution Agraire en Algérie. Historique, contenu et problèmes. 84 pp. 1978. ISBN 91-7106-145-2 (OUT-OF-PRINT)

48. Bhagavan, M.R., A Critique of "Appropriate" Technology for Underdeveloped Countries. 56 pp. 1979. SEK 45,-. ISBN 91-7106-150-9

49. Bhagavan, M.R., Inter-Relations Between Technological Choices and Industrial Strategies in Third World Countries. 79 pp. 1979. SEK 45,-. ISBN 91-7106-151-7

50. Torp, Jens Erik, Industrial Planning and Development in Mozambique. Some Preliminary Considerations. 59 pp. 1979. ISBN 91-7106-153-3 (OUT-OF-PRINT)

51. Brandström, Per, Jan Hultin & Jan Lindström, Aspects of Agro-Pastoralism in East Africa. 60 pp. 1979. ISBN 91-7106-155-X (OUT OF PRINT)

52. Egerö, Bertil, Colonization and Migration. A Summary of Border-Crossing Movements in Tanzania before 1967. 45 pp. 1979. SEK 45,-. ISBN 91-7106-159-2

53. Simson, Howard, Zimbabwe—A Country Study. 138 pp. 1979. ISBN 91-7106-160-6 (OUT-OF-PRINT)

54. Beshir, Mohamed Omer, Diversity Regionalism and National Unity. 50 pp. 1979. ISBN 91-7106-166-5 (OUT-OF-PRINT)

55. Eriksen, Tore Linné, Modern African History: Some Historiographical Observations. 27 pp. 1979. ISBN 91-7106-167-3 (OUT OF PRINT)

56. Melander, Göran, Refugees in Somalia. 48 pp. 1980. SEK 45,-. ISBN 91-7106-169-X

57. Bhagavan, M.R., Angola: Prospects for Socialist Industrialisation. 48 pp. 1980. ISBN 91-7106-175-4 (OUT OF PRINT)

58. Green, Reginald H., From Südwestafrika to Namibia. The Political Economy of Transition. 45 pp. 1981. SEK 45,-. ISBN 91-7106-188-6

59. Isaksen, Jan, Macro-Economic Management and Bureaucracy: The Case of Botswana. 53 pp. 1981. SEK 45,-. ISBN 91-7106-192-4

60. Odén, Bertil, The Macroeconomic Position of Botswana. 84 pp. 1981. SEK 45,-. ISBN 91-7106-193-2

61. Westerlund, David, From Socialism to Islam? Notes on Islam as a Political Factor in Contemporary Africa. 62 pp. 1982. SEK 45,-. ISBN 91-7106-203-3

62. Tostensen, Arne, Dependence and Collective Self-Reliance in Southern Africa. The Case of the Southern African Development Coordination Conference (SADCC). 170 pp. 1982. ISBN 91-7106-207-6 (OUT-OF-PRINT)

63. Rudebeck, Lars, Problèmes de pouvoir populaire et de développement. Transition difficile en Guinée-Bissau. 73 pp. 1982. ISBN 91-7106-208-4 (OUT-OF-PRINT)

64. Nobel, Peter, Refugee Law in the Sudan. With The Refugee Conventions and The Regulation of Asylum Act of 1974. 56 pp. 1982. SEK 45,-. ISBN 91-7106-209-2

65. Sano, H-O, The Political Economy of Food in Nigeria 1960–1982. A Discussion on Peasants, State, and World Economy. 108 pp. 1983. ISBN 91-7106-210-6 (OUT-OF-PRINT)

66. Kjærby, Finn, Problems and Contradictions in the Development of Ox-Cultivation in Tanzania. 164 pp. 1983. SEK 60,-. ISBN 91-7106-211-4

67. Kibreab, Gaim, Reflections on the African Refugee Problem: A Critical Analysis of Some Basic Assumptions. 154 pp. 1983. ISBN 91-7106-212-2 (OUT-OF-PRINT) (

68. Haarløv, Jens, Labour Regulation and Black Workers' Struggles in South Africa. 80 pp. 1983. SEK 20,-. ISBN 91-7106-213-0

69. Matshazi, Meshack Jongilanga & Christina Tillfors, *A Survey of Workers' Education Activities in Zimbabwe, 1980–1981*. 85 pp. 1983. SEK 45,-. ISBN 91-7106-217-3

70. Hedlund, Hans & Mats Lundahl, *Migration and Social Change in Rural Zambia*. 107 pp. 1983. SEK 50,-. ISBN 91-7106-220-3

71. Gasarasi, Charles P., *The Tripartite Approach to the Resettlement and Integration of Rural Refugees in Tanzania*. 76 pp. 1984. SEK 45,-. ISBN 91-7106-222-X

72. Kameir, El-Wathig & I. Kursany, *Corruption as a "Fifth" Factor of Production in the Sudan*. 33 pp. 1985. SEK 45,-. ISBN 91-7106-223-8

73. Davies, Robert, *South African Strategy Towards Mozambique in the Post-Nkomati Period. A Critical Analysis of Effects and Implications*. 71 pp. 1985. SEK 45,-. ISBN 91-7106-238-6

74. Bhagavan, M.R. *The Energy Sector in SADCC Countries. Policies, Priorities and Options in the Context of the African Crisis*. 41 pp. 1985. SEK 45,-. ISBN 91-7106-240-8

75. Bhagavan, M.R. *Angola's Political Economy 1975–1985*. 89 pp. 1986. SEK 45,-. ISBN 91-7106-248-3

76. Östberg, Wilhelm, *The Kondoa Transformation. Coming to Ggrips with Soil Erosion in Central Tanzania*. 99 pp. 1986. ISBN 91-7106-251-3 (OUT OF PRINT)

77. Fadahunsi, Akin, *The Development Process and Technology. A Case for a Resources Based Development Strategy in Nigeria*. 41 pp. 1986. SEK 45,-. ISBN 91-7106-265-3

78. Suliman, Hassan Sayed, *The Nationalist Move ments in the Maghrib. A Comparative Approach*. 87 pp. 1987. SEK 45,-. ISBN 91-7106-266-1

79. Saasa, Oliver S., *Zambia's Policies towards Foreign Investment. The Case of the Mining and Non-Mining Sectors*. 65 pp. 1987. SEK 45,-. ISBN 91-7106-271-8

80. Andræ, Gunilla & Björn Beckman, *Industry Goes Farming. The Nigerian Raw Material Crisis and the Case of Textiles and Cotton*. 68 pp. 1987. SEK 50,-. ISBN 91-7106-273-4

81. Lopes, Carlos & Lars Rudebeck, *The Socialist Ideal in Africa. A Debate*. 27 pp. 1988. SEK 45,-. ISBN 91-7106-280-7

82. Hermele, Kenneth, *Land Struggles and Social Differentiation in Southern Mozambique. A Case Study of Chokwe, Limpopo 1950–1987*. 64 pp. 1988. SEK 50,- ISBN 91-7106-282-3

83. Smith, Charles David, *Did Colonialism Capture the Peasantry? A Case Study of the Kagera District, Tanza nia*. 34 pp. 1989. SEK 45,-. ISBN 91-7106-289-0

84. Hedlund, S. & M. Lundahl, *Ideology as a Deter minant of Economic Systems: Nyerere and Ujamaa in Tanzania*. 54 pp. 1989. SEK 50,-. ISBN 91-7106-291-2

85. Lindskog, Per & Jan Lundqvist, *Why Poor Children Stay Sick. The Human Ecology of Child Health and Welfare in Rural Malawi*. 111 pp. 1989. SEK 60,-. ISBN 91-7106-284-X

86. Holmén, Hans, *State, Cooperatives and Develop ment in Africa*. 87 pp. 1990. SEK 60,-. ISBN 91-7106-300-5

87. Zetterqvist, Jenny, *Refugees in Botswana in the Light of International Law*. 83 pp. 1990. SEK 60,-. ISBN 91-7106-304-8

88. Rwelamira, Medard, *Refugees in a Chess Game: Reflections on Botswana, Lesotho and Swaziland Refugee Policies*. 63 pp. 1990. SEK 60,-. ISBN 91-7106-306-4

89. Gefu, Jerome O., *Pastoralist Perspectives in Nigeria. The Fulbe of Udubo Grazing Reserve*. 106 pp. 1992. SEK 60,-. ISBN 91-7106-324-2

90. Heino, Timo-Erki, *Politics on Paper. Finland's South Africa Policy 1945–1991*. 121 pp. 1992. SEK 60,-. ISBN 91-7106-326-9

91. Eriksson, Gun, *Peasant Response to Price Incentives in Tanzania. A Theoretical and Empirical Investigation*. 84 pp. 1993. SEK 60,- . ISBN 91-7106-334-X

92. Chachage, C.S.L., Magnus Ericsson & Peter Gibbon, *Mining and Structural Adjustment. Studies on Zimbabwe and Tanzania*. 107 pp. 1993. SEK 60,-. ISBN 91-7106-340-4

93. Neocosmos, Michael, *The Agrarian Question in Southern Africa and "Accumulation from Below". Economics and Politics in the Struggle for Democracy*. 79 pp. 1993. SEK 60,-. ISBN 91-7106-342-0

94. Vaa, Mariken, *Towards More Appropriate Technologies? Experiences from the Water and Sanitation Sector*. 91 pp. 1993. SEK 60,-. ISBN 91-7106-343-9

95. Kanyinga, Karuti, Andrew Kiondo & Per Tidemand, *The New Local Level Politics in East Africa. Studies on Uganda, Tanzania and Kenya*. 119 pp. 1994. SEK 60,-. ISBN 91-7106-348-X

96. Odén, Bertil, H. Melber, T. Sellström & C. Tapscott. *Namibia and External Resources. The Case of Swedish Development Assistance*. 122 pp. 1994. SEK 60,-. ISBN 91-7106-351-X

97. Moritz, Lena, *Trade and Industrial Policies in the New South Africa*. 61 pp. 1994. SEK 60,-. ISBN 91-7106-355-2

98. Osaghae, Eghosa E., *Structural Adjustment and Ethnicity in Nigeria*. 66 pp. 1995. SEK 60,-. ISBN 91-7106-373-0

99. Soiri, Iina, *The Radical Motherhood. Namibian Women's Independence Struggle*. 115 pp. 1996. SEK 60,-. ISBN 91-7106-380-3.

100. Rwebangira, Magdalena K., *The Legal Status of Women and Poverty in Tanzania*. 58 pp. 1996. SEK 60,-. ISBN 91-7106-391-9

101. Bijlmakers, Leon A., Mary T. Bassett & David M. Sanders, *Health and Structural Adjustment in Rural and Urban Zimbabwe*. 78 pp. 1996. SEK 60,-. ISBN 91-7106-393-5

102. Gibbon, Peter & Adebayo O. Olukoshi, *Structural Adjustment and Socio-Economic Change in Sub-Saharan Africa. Some Conceptual,*

Methodological and Research Issues. 101 pp. 1996. SEK 80,-. ISBN 91-7106-397-8

103. Egwu, Samuel G., *Structural Adjustment, Agrarian Change and Rural Ethnicity in Nigeria.* 124 pp. 1998. SEK 80,-. ISBN 91-7106-426-5

104. Olukoshi, Adebayo O., *The Elusive Prince of Denmark. Structural Adjustment and the Crisis of Governance in Africa.* 59 pp. 1998. SEK 80,-. ISBN 91-7106-428-1

105. Bijlmakers, Leon A., Mary T. Bassett & David M. Sanders, *Socioeconomic Stress, Health and Child Nutritional Status in Zimbabwe at a Time of Economic Structural Adjustment. A Three Year Longitudinal Study.* 127 pp. 1998. SEK 80,-. ISBN 91-7106-434-6

106. Mupedziswa, Rodrick and Perpetua Gumbo, *Structural Adjustment and Women Informal Sector Traders in Harare, Zimbabwe.* 123 pp. 1998. SEK 80,-. ISBN 917106-435-4

107. Chiwele, D.K., P. Muyatwa-Sipula and H. Kalinda, *Private Sector Response to Agricultural Marketing Liberalisation in Zambia. A Case Study of Eastern Provice Maize Markets.* 90 pp. SEK 80,-. ISBN 91-7106-436-2

108. Amanor, K.S., *Global Restructuring and Land Rights in Ghana. Forest Food Chains, Timber and Rural Livelihoods.* 154 pp. 1999. SEK 80,-. ISBN 91-7106-437-0

109. Ongile, G.A., *Gender and Agricultural Supply Responses to Structural Adjustment Programmes. A Case Study of Smallholder Tea Producers in Kericho, Kenya.* 91 pp. 1999. SEK 80,- ISBN 91-7106-440-0

110. Sachikonye, Lloyd M., *Restructuring or De-Industrializing? Zimbabwe's Textile and Metal Industries under Structural Adjustment.* 107 pp. 1999. SEK 100,-. ISBN 91-7106-444-3

111. Gaidzanwa, Rudo, *Voting with their Feet. Migrant Zimbabwean Nurses and Doctors in the Era of Structural Adjustment.* 84 pp. 1999. SEK 100,-. ISBN 91-7106-445-1

112. Andersson, Per-Åke, Arne Bigsten and Håkan Persson, *Foreign Aid, Debt and Growth in Zambia.* 133 pp. 2000. SEK 100,-. ISBN 91-7106-462-1

113. Hashim, Yahaya and Kate Meagher, *Cross-Border Trade and the Parallel Currency Market —Trade and Finance in the Context of Structural Adjustment. A Case Study from Kano, Nigeria.* 118 pp. 1999. SEK 100,-. ISBN 91-7106-449-4

114. Schlyter, Ann, *Recycled Inequalitites. Youth and gender in George compound, Zambia,* 135 pp. 1999. SEK 100,-. ISBN 91-7106-455-9

115. Kanyinga, Karuti, *Re-Distribution from Above. The Politics of Land Rights and Squatting in Coastal Kenya.* 126 pp. 2000. SEK 100,-. ISBN 91-7106-464-8

116. Amanor, Kojo Sebastian, *Land, Labour and the Family in Southern Ghana. A Critique of Land Policy under Neo-Liberalisation.* 127 pp. 2001. SEK 100,-. ISBN 91-7106-468-0